THE DEEP HEART'S CORE

First published in 2017 by
The Dedalus Press
13 Moyclare Road
Baldoyle
Dublin D13 K1C2
Ireland

www.**dedaluspress**.com

Foreword copyright © Bernard O'Donoghue, 2017
Introductions copyright © Eugene O'Connell
& Pat Boran respectively, 2017
This selection copyright © Dedalus Press, 2017
All poems and prose commentaries copyright © their respective
authors. The Acknowledgements section (pp. 315 to 317) shall be
understood to constitute an extension of this copyright notice.

ISBN 978 1 910251 18 8 (paperback)
ISBN 978 1 910251 19 5 (hardback)

Cover image: iStock.com/aroas
Typesetting & Design: Pat Boran

Dedalus Press titles are represented in the UK by
Inpress Ltd., *www.inpressbooks.co.uk*
and in North America by Syracuse University Press, Inc.,
www.syracuseuniversitypress.syr.edu

Dedalus Press receives financial assistance from
The Arts Council / An Chomhairle Ealaíon.

THE DEEP HEART'S CORE

Irish Poets Revisit
A Touchstone Poem

Edited by
**Eugene O'Connell
& Pat Boran**

Foreword by
Bernard O'Donoghue

DEDALUS PRESS

THANKS

Grateful acknowledgment is made to all of the authors, publishers, agents and representatives for permission to include copyright material in this anthology. Detailed acknowledgements may be found on pp. 315 to 317.

CONTENTS

THE POEMS

CONTENTS

7

Foreword

BERNARD O'DONOGHUE

⁓

Ours is a great age of poetry readings; we have all had the experience of enlightenment when something we hadn't grasped is explained by the reading poet. Often we feel 'It would not have been possible to know that on the page, without the poet's presence'.

Eugene O'Connell's brilliant idea here is to transfer the presence of the reading poet on to the page. Just as poets at a reading choose their own preferred work, and can say what they like about it, here they can exercise exactly the same freedom on the page. We find out how much biography the poet wants the reader to have; in several of the essays here the poets return to the question of 'confessionalism': how much of the writer's own life they want to be explicit for the reader. But we learn other things too: as with Keats's letters, we find out what the writer's view of poetry is — what it is for. Edna Longley once said that all worthwhile poems have something to say about poetry. The poems here are personal, political, formally strict or free, according to the writer's view of the art.

O'Connell says in his introduction, "This anthology might double as an introduction to Irish poetry for the general reader and as a handbook for the aspiring student or practitioner." The book is certainly a wonderfully full and various snapshot of

Irish poetry at a particular time in its illustrious history. And it shows Irish poetry to be in very good form: engaged, confident and accomplished — as you would expect, given that the writers are choosing their best and most representative work. It is a marvellous showcase for them.

Defining Vision

EUGENE O'CONNELL

～

While editing the *Cork Literary Review* some years ago I asked a selection of poets — some of whom are no longer with us — to choose a poem of their own that seemed to encapsulate their own particular 'voice' or vision and to explore in prose why they regarded that poem as seminal to their overall work.

That first small section grew over time into the present anthology that represents, hopefully, the many strands and voices that today make up Irish poetry.

Though I have had second thoughts since about the notion that a single poem might embody an individual 'voice' or sensibility (how does one define vision!), I was struck by the reaction of the poets to my request; how they instinctively recognised that one particular poem which could be a watershed event in their writing life, a moment of realisation ("I dabbled in verse and it became my life," as Patrick Kavanagh had it.)

The honesty of their replies, and the frankness with which they spoke of quite sensitive personal matters, took me by surprise. The urgency of their response was curiously affirming.

A number of factors emerged as common ground in the creative process: the trigger for the original impulse; the vision that slowly reveals itself, evolving over time; the awareness of a formative moment in the evolution of the art. (Michael Coady, for example, talks of "being bitten by the bug", on hearing his father recite.)

What struck me as I read each of the pieces was how central in the life of the writer poetry is, how contemplation of it is balm for the soul (one poet tells of how she rarely writes poetry now but thinks continually about the craft), how poetry offers solace in an increasingly secular world, a way of reclaiming language appropriated by commerce for its own ends.

These poems and short essays afford a snapshot of what is being written in a particular time and place, a flavour of what drives poets in their explorations and persuades them ultimately to offer those explorations to a wider readership.

This anthology might double as an introduction to Irish poetry for the general reader and as a handbook for the aspiring student or practitioner. From the viewpoint of gender alone, one notices various features and patterns: how the female and male contributors appear drawn to particular themes and subjects, the tone of voice employed, the subtle differences and variations of diction and technique.

In relation to what might be called the pathology of the creative impulse — a motif I hadn't expected to emerge — one might ask is there a link between the creative impulse and mania? Can the practise of poetry heighten anxiety, unhinge an addictive personality?

Whatever else it is, this volume will be seen as a unique and illuminating compendium of poets from Ireland (most natives, many more recent arrivals or long-term visitors) stopping to look back, even briefly, at their own work. As such, it is mercifully free of navel-gazing, yet it doesn't shirk from recognising the widest possible range of personal and public concerns.

The Gaps Between Poems

PAT BORAN

Among the often overlooked attractions of the poetry reading are, paradoxically, the words not written down, the words not scrubbed to within an inch of their lives and put on display in their Sunday best for all to admire. In the gaps between the poems, one might say, even the most casual introductory remarks of the poet may illuminate some aspect of the work.

Tellingly, this is true both for those who read from the page and for those who recite from memory. It is as if, reunited with their work far from the place and time of its composition (and now in the presence of a live audience), poets often find themselves seeing from a perspective other than their own. Like singers singing familiar songs they are both practitioners and, once again, members of the audience. Whether on stage in the local pub or at a major literary festival, therefore, it is not uncommon to hear poets noticing things in their poems that up to now have entirely escaped their attention. When I interviewed poets on radio for some years, it was often that moment where they found themselves simultaneously 'inside' and 'outside' of their work that most interested me.

Of course, in its simplest form, the practice of poets introducing or commenting on their own work is merely a recognition of the need to engage, to lift one's head even briefly from the page (or depart from the memorized script) and make meaningful contact in the moment. For this reason the 'small talk' of the typical poetry reading may also exist as a welcome counterpoint to the more intense language of poetry itself. Though poems must be entire of themselves — and poets should beware the temptation to paraphrase or explain — the opportunity to highlight matters of form or subject matter, the circumstances of composition, etc. is one that few poets, and even fewer audiences, pass up on.

Many poets say they have favourite reading poems, poems that invariably 'go down well' in a live setting. But if some poems work better than others (being more easily absorbed or comprehended), then the permission to 'frame' less immediately revealing work with some introductory remarks may permit a wider range of expression and ensure that the public gathering is worthwhile in itself and not simply a diluted version of a more meaningful private engagement.

Which brings me to our title. *The Deep Heart's Core* comes, of course, from Yeats' 'The Lake Isle of Innisfree'. (For those who haven't heard it, there's a wonderful recording of the poet reciting — or declaiming — the poem, which, as it happens, he introduces with a brief note on its composition.) Though firmly set in the rural Co. Sligo of his childhood visits, this most famous Irish poem started to find form, Yeats tells us, in a London of "pavements grey", in fact on a day when he stood for some time looking into a shop window where a small water ornament reminded him of the "lake water lapping" of that far-off world of Innisfree. It required that moment of pause, that recognition of a somewhat grim present for his childhood idyll to assume its distinctly mythic power and set the poem in motion.

A similar relationship between triggering impulse and final text is what we're drawn to in this volume. Some poets recall a place and time of inspiration, others consider any of a range of formal elements ranging from an itch of rhythm to an initial stitch of rhyme. But as anyone with even a passing interest in the subject knows, the potency, the depth of poetry — however and wherever we first encounter it — only truly begins to lay claim to our hearts over subsequent returns.

GRAHAM ALLEN

Military Hill

What do you want?
What would you have wanted?

I see you sometimes in the street,
I did not mean to keep you unborn.

You are playing football.
You have brown eyes and a hurt nose.

You are running for your life.
I cannot help you.

From this distance you have no name.
You burn in the palm of my hand.

You stand, unseen, outside of every window.
We did not hear you calling,

or you yourself were deaf.
But we need you now,

Cork boy with matted hair,
a toy gun and torn trousers,

kicking cans down Military Hill,
madly excited about tomorrow.

I have lived the majority of the twenty-one years I've been
in Cork around the St. Luke's / Wellington Road / Military
Hill area of the city. I have written a number of poems

now which reflect on this area. This poem 'Military Hill' is characteristic in that its theme is, finally, the future. The boy imagined was always there at the back of my mind. A young person that may one day materially arrive. Since writing the poem I have been blest with the most wonderful son, Matthew, whom I cannot help connecting with the boy addressed in the poem, even though the poem was written a few years before his birth. Military Hill is of course a road that leads up to what was once the British Army and is now the Irish Army barracks. There is a lot of history around about that road and a good deal of it is not good. The boy, however, at the end of the poem is running away from that past and is occupied with the pleasures and the possibilities of today and the days to come. He is my figure for hope since hope is always located somewhere in the future that may yet arrive. It is characteristic of what I write, I hope, to argue that the meaning we seek for our lives lies most genuinely in what might still arrive rather than what has already happened. This poem seems to be popular with those who are familiar with my work and I'd like to think it was this aspect of it, rather than the somewhat uncharacteristic confessional tone, that they appreciate. I may of course be mistaken in this.

TARA BERGIN

This is Yarrow

In this country house I had a dream of the city
as if the thick yarrow heads had told me,
as if the chokered dove had told me,
or the yellow elder seeds had made me ask —
and in the dream I went up to the dirty bus station
and I saw the black side of the power station
and as if the brown moth's tapping at the window
made me say it I said, do you still love me?
And when I woke and went to the window,
your tender voice told me: this is yarrow,
this is elder, this is the collared dove.

'This is Yarrow' was one of the first poems I ever published. It appeared in *Poetry London* in 2007 and would eventually become the title poem of my first collection. Towards the end of the poem there is a very ordinary line: 'do you still love me?' and you could argue that it's really too ordinary to include in a poem. But it has a secret importance to me. This line comes from a postcard sent in 1926 by the Russian writer Marina Tsvetaeva. She was writing to the German poet, Rainer Maria Rilke, unaware that he was mortally ill. They had only been corresponding for a few months and had never met in person. Having received no answer to her last letter, the postcard she sent simply contained the following message: 'Dear Rainer, This is where I live. I wonder if you still love me?' A month later, Tsvetaeva heard that Rilke had died. Devastated, she wrote to Pasternak to tell him the news, misquoting herself by saying that she had written to Rilke *'Rainer, was ist? Rainer, liebst Du mich noch?'* (Rainer, what is it? Rainer, do you love me still?). It's a bold, crazy thing to write to someone you've never met, and captures that alarmingly direct, over-possessive — but at the same time throwaway — tone of much of Tsvetaeva's work. This appealed to me greatly. It seemed to carry the sense of a poor quality long distance phone call, in which only the most important, urgent instructions can be conveyed: all else is superfluous. I recognised in this a mood of yearning and desperation that was in keeping with many of the poems I was writing at that time.

EAVAN BOLAND

That the Science of Cartography is Limited

— and not simply by the fact that this shading of
forest cannot show the fragrance of balsam,
the gloom of cypresses
is what I wish to prove.

When you and I were first in love we drove
to the borders of Connacht
and entered a wood there.

Look down you said: this was once a famine road.

I looked down at ivy and the scutch grass
rough-cast stone had
disappeared into as you told me
in the second winter of their ordeal, in

1847, when the crop had failed twice,
Relief Committees gave
the starving Irish such roads to build.

Where they died, there the road ended

and ends still and when I take down
the map of this island, it is never so
I can say here is
the masterful, the apt rendering of

the spherical as flat, nor
an ingenious design which persuades a curve
into a plane,
but to tell myself again that

the line which says woodland and cries hunger
and gives out among sweet pine and cypress,
and finds no horizon

will not be there.

The poem here — 'That the Science of Cartography is Limited' — was begun one January afternoon in Dublin. It was less difficult to finish than other poems of mine. Once it was done I could follow it back to another narrative: a crisscrossing of memory and decision and private history.

There were no maps in our house when I was growing up, none that I remember. At least not in the obvious places where I saw them in other houses — on the walls, framed, or as pages open on a table. If there were I have no image of them. But there were maps at school. I went to a convent just north of London, beginning there a few weeks late when I was six years of age. I continued there till I was eleven.

On the wall in one classroom was a map. The cracked textile unrolled from a wooden bar. I came back to the same classroom at different ages and for different classes: for history, for science, for English, for religion. I got used to seeing the greenish linen seas edging up to big coral territories.

This poem begins — or at least I intended it to — where maps fail. I built the proposition — that the science of cartography is limited — into the title because I wanted the poem to begin with a mouthful of reason and argument.

But the subject matter is not rational. The famine roads of 1847, required strength from those who had none. They were made in terrible circumstances. They are a mark of the time, a scar tissue of our history. And yet these roads don't turn up on any map. Their physicality, for all its suffering and significance, could not be measured by cartography — providing evidence, as the poem would argue, for the failure of that science.

DERMOT BOLGER

While We Sleep

i.e. Roger Bolger Senior,
b: 17ᵗʰ May 1918, Wexford
d: 20ᵗʰ April 2011, Dublin

While we sleep they are slipping beyond our reach —
Our elderly parents, frail aunts, grandfathers —

They are dressing themselves, opening doors in the night,
Venturing out in search of the first home they possessed;

Padding across motorway intersections in slippers in the dark,
Shuffling past shopping centres, hulls of lit-up office blocks.

We may be scared but they know where they are voyaging
Amid their endless confusion as to whether it is night or day,

Amid the terror they feel as they sense their brains capsizing,
They are walking back towards the reassurance of first memory:

The bedrock which for decades got obscured by pressing
    concerns,
Preoccupied with the business of surviving the business of life.

But now the clutter of middle years has been hacked away,
Reunited with themselves, unhurriedly, with vision unimpaired,

They are shuffling their way back to the streets of their birth,
Skirting carriageways, concourses, each neon-lit underpass.

They are any age and yet they have grown beyond age,
They have become absences in our lives, demanding our care,

Yet at the same time oblivious to us. We confuse them,
Disconnected from the landscape in which they are young.

We see shrunken figures in dressing gowns on Zimmer frames
But they are children sent to do a message, an errand of trust.

How can my father be ninety-two as he walks through the Faythe,
Knocking on neighbours' doors, stopping cloth-capped strangers,

Sent out to seek the loan of a good book for my grandfather to
    read:
A novel with sufficient heft and depth and intelligence to distract

A compositor sick of back proofing racks of letterpress newsprint,
Who wants to lose himself in a journey through unfamiliar
    streets?

A quiet man who would be led astray by old age into the
    County Home,
Where he waited for the books he sent his young son to seek
    years before.

Gentle grandfather, Republican typesetter, drinker on Ram Street,
Your vigil is over at the barred window of that Enniscorthy
    asylum,

Your son is coming with your treasured copy of *The Observer*
That he dutifully collects from the Dublin train every Sunday
    morning,

With a Canon Sheehan novel, with H.G. Wells and Chesterton,
With Charles Dickens, Edgar Allen Poe and Patrick McGill,

He got distracted from his errand during decades in ships' cabins,
Grieving his wife's death, becoming a connoisseur of loneliness.

But now he emerges through the far side of such struggles,
He has left his front door open, every light on deck aglow,

He shuffles on a busted hip, clutching a vast armful of books,
Knowing only that somewhere between Finglas and Wexford,

Between the century of his birth and the one where he dies
He will encounter his father, equally ancient, equally young.

His father will be pleased with the books, the errand fulfilled.
So while we fret for him adrift in such dangerous depths,

Unable to steer between tides of remembrance and despair,
A part of him siphons free from the confused husk who phones

Moments after we leave his house to ask why nobody ever comes:
The part that walks, beyond our remit, towards his dead father.

Even if we could follow them, they would be too engrossed to
    care
For the distraction of strangers like us who are not yet even
    born:

We would be intruding on a father and a son strolling back
    from town
To the Green Street terrace that is the first and last home they
    share.

There are certain duties that every son must do for his
father; to run childhood errands at the age when you
utterly depend upon them, and then — if they live long
enough — to realise that a time has come when they are now as
dependent upon you as you once were upon them.

My father was a seafarer who survived German aircraft attacks with the Wexford Steam Packet; storms, shipwrecks and sinkings. He was widowed early and lived an independent life into his ninetieth year. But then, gradually he lost his sense of time as his brain capsized and he retreated back to the Wexford streets of his birth, when his own father used to send him as a boy out on an errand each Friday evening to find a good book to read. He also had to walk down to meet the Dublin train every Sunday, on which Easons sent down his father's ordered copy of *The Observer* newspaper, which my grandfather was the only person in the town to read.

I wrote this poem when he was just starting to slip into dementia and he told me of a dream he had just had in which he was a boy again, having been sent off through Wexford by his father to find a good book to read but had been unable to find anyone who would loan him one.

Like most poets, I am probably the worst judge of my own poems. Therefore I picked this poem not so much because it is a touchstone poem for me but because it seems to affect many people at readings who relate it to someone in their own family who had undergone a similar journey, and therefore I find people regularly coming up to me afterwards to ask for a copy of it.

I suppose the poem is for anyone who has witnessed a loved one's slow deterioration and watched a fiercely independent person succumb to old age, where events of sixty years ago are more real than events today. In 2011 my brother Roger and I completed the last duty that any son can do for his father, when traffic was halted on the main street of Finglas village to allow us to carry his coffin across the hushed road and into St. Canice's Church.

PAT BORAN

Waving

As a child I waved to people I didn't know.
I waved from passing cars, school buses,
second floor windows, or from the street
to secretaries trapped in offices above.
When policemen motioned my father on
past the scene of the crime or an army checkpoint,
I waved back from the back seat. I loved to wave.
I saw the world disappear into a funnel
of perspective, like the reflection in the bath
sucked into a single point when the water drains.
I waved at things that vanished into points.
I waved to say, 'I see you: can you see me?'

I loved the 'notion of an ocean' that could wave,
of a sea that rose up to see the onlooker
standing on the beach. And, though the sea
came towards the beach, it was a different sea
when it arrived; the onlooker too had changed.
They disappeared, both of them, into points in time.
So that was why they waved to one another.
On the beach I waved until my arms hurt.

My mother waved her hair sometimes. This,
I know, seems to be something else.
But when she came up the street, bright and radiant,
her white hair like a jewel-cap on her head,
I waved and she approached me, smiling shyly.
Sometimes someone walking beside her might
wave back, wondering where they knew me from.
Hands itched in pockets, muscles twitched
when I waved. 'There's someone who sees me!'

But in general people took no risk with strangers,
and when they saw who I was — or wasn't —
they seemed relieved, saved from terrible disgrace.

Now it turns out that light itself is a wave
(as well as a point, or points), so though for me
the waving is done, it's really only just beginning.
Whole humans — arms, legs, backs and bellies —
are waving away, flickering on and off,
in and out of time and space;
pushing through streets with their heads down,
smiling up at office windows,
lying in gutters with their kneecaps broken
and their hopes dashed; driving, loving,
hiding, growing old, but always waving,
waving as if to say: 'Can you see me?
I can see you. Still … still … still …'

A good deal of what I write has its roots, its triggering impulse at least, in autobiography. Even so, it is never enough for a poem to exist as autobiography alone; it's never enough simply to communicate the facts, the atmosphere, or the effect of an individual happening, however interesting that happening might be.

While the details are of fundamental importance (and the poem can only earth itself through them) the poem has to go beyond or at least point beyond individual experience towards something larger than itself. By burrowing down, it reaches up; by going in, it extends outwards. In theory, at least.

For me the most successful poems, or at least the ones I feel retain some kind of life beyond the facts of their inception, are those that, in their writing, uncover some external form or pattern, some matrix or hook that was not apparent when the writing began. This can be a connected sequence of images, a dominant sound or rhythm or, with luck, all three.

In the initial impulse to get things down, a certain amount of blindness is not only good, but necessary. For 'Waving', I wrote the first line, then the next, and so on, without much planning. Things began to be clear only *because* I was writing. (Writing, and particularly revision, are ways to make sense of the world — or the world of a poem, at least.)

'Waving' is a poem that plays with (riffs on) the idea that light exhibits the properties of both wave and particle, depending on how it is viewed and measured. In a way the poem might be a metaphor for autobiography-based writing itself; it is a reminder to the poet in me that when I am most in control I may not be at my most perceptive, and vice versa.

There are a number of 'givens' in the text (some facts about my childhood, some basic understanding of a notorious scientific conundrum). And, as it is a relatively old poem now, there are many things I would do differently (if not to say better) if I had it to do over again. But for the most part what I like about it still is that, in the end, all these elements lead towards uncertainty, towards a mystery which, autobiographical or not, seems essential to a good poem, whoever it comes from, however it comes.

EVA BOURKE

Evening near Letterfrack

I'd brought the papers into the house, the saddest
stories for years, newsprint wet from rain or was it tears
blackened my hands and now I watched the mountains —
old herd of nags — lower themselves around the bay,
hippodrome-style. The sky was clearing, islands reappeared.
Clare Island, Bofin, Inishturk and way out High Island
seesawed among the breakers. Fast forward breezes
shook quaking grass, sorrel, colt's foot, rhododendrons
fuchsia shrubs, the rustling of some broad-leafed bush
sounded as if a score of blades were being sharpened.
Out near the strand a rock, a fossilized cetacean
was inch by inch submerging in the rising tide.
A feather of a cloud in the sheer sky withstood
the inroads of two transatlantic vapour trails
for longer than two minutes. Dog bark and pheasant call,
a donkey heehawed like a rusty barn door hinge
and on the trade routes of the birds
the evening traffic went on, swift and purposeful.
Such clarity of air, voices were carried far across
from a sandy beach beside the pier. Two women
walked the tidemark together in complete intimacy
picking up flotsam, stones and shells, the keepsakes
of a day they wanted to remember.
The one, young, black, wore a Nubian crown
of plaited locks, the other's head shone in the evening light
like weathered driftwood, smooth, bleached and silvered.
They talked as friend to friend, mother to daughter,
old to young, black to white. Two dogs were chasing
one another around them in the tidal surf.
Where were divisions now? The line between
the water and the sky, all binaries and opposites

dissolved here at the end of Europe
among the quartzite stones and soft black bog.
Don't be afraid, someone sang in the distance,
and *I'll stay with you!*
The air was brimful of avowals and annunciations.

'Evening near Letterfrack' arose out of circumstance as is so often the case with poems. We were spending a few days in the cottage of friends not far from Letterfrack on the Renvyle peninsula, having just returned from a longer stay abroad.

It was the 20th of May, the day the Ryan Report was published in *The Irish Times*, with typical West of Ireland weather, changeable, stormy, with driving clouds, showers and intermittent sun. I had been reading the paper outside during a sunny spell and, when the showers returned, the pages of the report were sodden by the time I got back to the house.

My reactions to the report were initially — probably like most people's — a wild mixture of shock, disbelief, rage and sorrow. I had read Mannix Flynn's powerful autobiographical novel about his years of physical and sexual abuse at the hands of the brothers in the industrial school in Letterfrack, so I wasn't entirely unprepared.

But I could not foresee the emotional impact of the account with its dispassionate diction which seemed to highlight the savagery and which went on and on, listing in great detail the sufferings of countless children in orphanages and industrial schools run by the Catholic Church across Ireland. Letterfrack industrial school, where one hundred and forty-seven children died before it was closed in 1974, has become a metonymy for the brutal regimes in these institutions.

But there are other histories connected with Letterfrack, for example that of James and Mary Ellis, a Quaker couple who arrived in the middle of the 19th century from England to help with the post-Famine relief. According to the Quaker maxim *Thou shalt not judge,* they simply set about providing land, housing, schooling and work for the impoverished community without any attempt at proselytising.

Another narrative is that of the unique festivals that have taken place there — Sea Week and Bog Week organised by Clare and Leo Hallissey — which have drawn natural scientists, environmentalists, artists, musicians and poets to Letterfrack for the past thirty years, fostering enjoyment of the beautiful but fragile natural environment of Connemara among the wider community of this remote peninsula.

The poem is divided into two eighteen-line sections without a visible break. In the first eighteen lines of the poem physical events reflect the emotions — nature is invested with or seems to correlate to the inner turmoil of the speaker who is looking out at the sea, watching the high waves and observing the wind rake through seaside grasses and shrubs.

There is a gradual modulation, a subsiding of the turbulence as the sky clears and nature returns to calmer everyday protocols. A brief caesura after purposeful at the end of the eighteenth line leads over to the interjection: "Such clarity of air", after which the mood of the poem begins to change from a minor to a major key, as it were, building up towards the epiphany of the natural deconstruction of all binary dichotomies and power relationships embodied in the very materials of the landscape and enacted by the two women in the strand.

And although the position of the speaker remains that of the onlooker who isn't taking sides, perhaps in observance of the Quaker maxim, the verbal promise in the last two lines is explicitly inclusive and without exception.

HEATHER BRETT

Bankrupt

for my son Greg 1981–2008

I eat the last of the white peaches from Sedona.
Delicate inlay of texture and taste.
The sun hasn't quite reached this window yet
but the patio is alive; tiny prehistoric,
long-thin-tailed lizards that jack
and pump themselves on the brickwork;
bees hover and burrow in the lemon rose of the cacti
and stripped agave amid the creosote
pushes its spikes skyward,
pierces the shadow of a turkey vulture,
its wings outstretched, feathers spread,
rifling the sizzling air.
Glint of blue-green-black butterfly flap,
crickets that pulse and trill from the milkweed.
And I think of that particular point where one stops
watching, stops listening,
folds back the formed word on the tongue, stops feeling:
and I wonder how long I've been sitting here
a study in loss, but breathing.

A residency in Oracle, Pinal County, Arizona. Monsoon month when rattlers, scorpions and tarantulas move about after the downpours. Vibrancy upped a notch. Scorched Sonoran Desert earth, an exotic, rugged beauty in the cacti, lavish landscape and wildlife, raw power in granite mountains, incredible starry skies. Yet I felt it was a place removed, or maybe that man cannot really touch it. We will come and go, it will last, weather-beaten, forever, and has the power to destroy us.

Like loss, a scouring of the soul, we continue, yet what an empty thing we are. The death of my son gouged any remaining impetus. When the world still held wonder, before my daughter died, was a long, long time ago.

Yet, it's an incredible, wondrous place this earth, our lives as full as we make them — or not.

'Bankrupt' had little editing … I loved it for its honesty, the juxtaposition of such a flourishing existence with nothing.

PADDY BUSHE

After Love

for Fíona

The cockle relaxes its grip. Small creatures,
Like nerves on the estuary of our bodies,
Settle again, and discover once more
Their oozing world, as the tide recedes.

The frantic seaweed, stilled now,
Only half regrets the small rivulets
Still trickling, unpractised, towards the sea.
The small salt-grassed islands can forget

The surge and swell that joined them
And go back to just being islands,
For the time being, and the space being,
To ring and ring and ring in silence.

A lark is climbing through octaves of the sky
To celebrate us, high and dry.

Around 1982, I was in my mid-thirties, and hadn't written a poem since I was a student in the late '60s. I was happily settled in South Kerry with my wife and young children, and had concluded that my youthful belief that I would be a poet had been a pleasant but fruitless interlude.

And then, out of nowhere that I was aware of, the sonnet 'After Love' more or less dreamed itself into being during an exhilarated post-coital doze early one morning. I got up, and with minimal effort, shaped the poem into its present form.

I don't think any other poem I ever wrote had anything like such an easy passage. And somehow the easy passage it enjoyed gave me back my lost confidence. I must have been subconsciously yearning for some such stimulus.

In any event, I have been writing since; for better or worse must remain for others to judge. But it is not only the debt of gratitude I owe to the poem which makes it significant for me. It is also that 'After Love' presaged some of the characteristics of my work which have remained. The poem is a celebration of the love that has animated so much of my poetry.

It is also rooted in a very particular place, in this case the enclosed tidal estuary of the Inny River beside where I live. A reader is not and need not be aware of this, but this specific locating of poems is primary to my work, and I can trace most of my poems, be they personal, political, historical or whatever, to a particular place, often at a particular time, even when the location itself is written out of the poem.

In this poem the identification of the lovers, body and soul, with the estuary, its creatures and its vegetation during an ebbing tide, came in a dream. Usually the process is more conscious, more worked and more difficult. Other characteristics also established themselves, I think: a hankering after shape and form, an affirmation of the lyric and an eschewal of ironic self-protection.

But I have begun to tread in areas best left to the judgement of others, and will let the poem speak for itself, thirty-five years after it was written.

Crab Apples

There used to be skylarks, he said:
we would lie
on the flat of our backs
in summer, to listen,
and in the hedgerows,
crab apples.

But the fifty acre field
grows no hedgerows where
birds might flutter and perch;
no corncrake rasps to break
the still air above
the sileaged grass,
and the skylark's song
no longer tumbles
to the fields and woods
round Ringabella.

This early poem follows a conversation I had with an immediate neighbour. I had just moved to Ringabella, a peninsula jutting into the sea from the southwest corner of Cork harbour, and was learning the lore of the place as I settled in.

Ringabella was arable land: its fields criss-crossed hillocks that dipped towards the sea. It was moving towards industrial-style farming, and the fields were becoming even larger to accommodate the huge machines that worked them. Hedges that had given shelter, and defined the amount that a man and his horse could work during a day, had become an inconvenience, and were being removed. Farmers themselves had become rare birds, perched high on tractors or concealed in 4x4s as they herded cattle; instead those who depended on the city for work, like myself, had moved in to walk the fields and lanes. For us the country had nothing to do with work, but was somewhere we escaped its pressures, a primordial battery where we plugged ourselves in for free and recharged.

'Crab Apples' records not just the loss of a skylark's song, but the passing of an age. Ways of speaking were part of that, and the poetry of the ordinary speech around me struck me then, and remains important to me now. The first words in the poem were my neighbour's, and snatches of conversation often appear in my later work, for example in the long poem based on my experience of Irish prisons, *The Island* ("where's her copybook? — Miss, her copybook / is all covered in blood"). 'Crab Apples' was also where I experimented with sound and rhyme, and discovered that I could construct a musical progression of vowels, like notes going down a musical scale, to lead towards the end of a poem.

MOYA CANNON

Chauvet

for John Berger

One red line, defining his rump,
draws the small mammoth out of the cave wall,
renders him more than a stalagmite.

In another chamber,
a bear's paw protrudes,
outlined in charcoal.

The animals had been in the wall all along,
awaiting recognition, release.
The stone-age artists knew it,

just as the Italian master would know it,
as his chisel unlocked perfect forms
from Carrara's marble,

as we know it,
when some informed, deft gesture—
a tilt in a melody,
a lit line in a poem or a song—
draws us out into our humanity,
warm-blooded,
bewildered

I n 2004, I visited an exhibition called 'The Age of the Mammoths' in the Jardin des Plantes in Paris. The final item in the exhibition was a display case containing a number of small ivory carvings. Amongst them was a mammoth ivory horse from Vogelherd, Germany, less than five centimetres long, dated at about 30,000 B.C., and claiming to be the world's oldest known sculpture*. The perfection of the little carved horse, the delicacy of expression in the head, the grace of the arched neck and back, the detail of the mane and tail totally undermined any stereotypical depiction of late stone-age man as being a mere club-wielder, intent on killing his next meal. The person who had carved this horse had skilled hands and a fine aesthetic sensibility. His or her powers of observation and empathy were like those of a present day Inuit sculptor. The hunter, like the artist, notices detail because he or she has to.

The Vogelherd horse recalled an article by John Berger, which I had read a few years previously. It was on the subject of paintings in the Chauvet Cave in France. The paintings had been discovered in 1995 and had been dated to approximately 30,000 — 32,000 B.C., many millennia earlier than the dates attributed to the wall paintings of Lascaux and Altamira. In his splendid article on the subject, Berger noted that the Stone Age artists had, in several cases, used protuberances and cavities in the walls as a basis for their drawings, as though they believed that the animals were inside the rock, that they required only a few strokes of red pigment to complete them. This reminded me of Michelangelo's claim that he was merely releasing sculptures from blocks of marble. It was as though the late stone-age artists were, in the other sense of the word, 'drawing' the animals out of the rock.

Berger commented that, although the Chauvet paintings predated those at Altamira and Lascaux by up to 15,000 years, they were mostly "as skilful, observant and graceful as any of the later paintings". (Iris Murdoch said something equivalent in relation to literature, "literature does not progress in the same way as the sciences. No one is better than Homer.") Berger also commented that the people who lived in the late Palaeolithic had music and jewellery. He wrote "Art, it would seem, is born

40

like a foal that can walk straight away … or, the talent to make art accompanies the need for that art; they arrive together."

The evidence suggests that the need to make something beautiful was central to our emergence as human beings, that it perhaps even defined us as human beings. Our need for beauty is very old. It is impossible to imagine a human society which does not cultivate at least one branch of the arts. But art must be accurate if it is to keep faith with the realities of our existence. In the writing of the poem, I was reminded of how vitally important, on an individual level, music, song, story and visual art are in our own personal emergence and integration, at adolescence and later. The pleasure of making something beautiful, or of experiencing it, brings into dialogue conflicting aspects of our humanity and allows us to feel more vibrantly alive, allows us to somehow emerge from the wall.

*Since 2004, mammoth ivory sculptures with significantly earlier radiocarbon dates have been identified.

CIARAN CARSON

Turn Again

There is a map of the city which shows the bridge that was
      never built.
A map which shows the bridge that collapsed; the streets that
      never existed.
Ireland's Entry, Elbow Lane, Weigh-House Lane, Back Lane,
      Stone-Cutter's Entry —
Today's plan is already yesterday's — the streets that were there
      are gone.
And the shape of the jails cannot be shown for security
      reasons.

The linen backing is falling apart — the Falls Road hangs
      by a thread.
When someone asks me where I live, I remember where I used
      to live.
Someone asks me for directions, and I think again. I turn into
A side street to try to throw off my shadow, and history
      is changed.

'Turn Again' is the first poem in my book *Belfast Confetti*, published in 1989. I don't remember anything much about the poem's genesis, or when exactly it was written in the late 1980s. I have to turn to Wiki to check how fraught a period that was in the Northern Ireland Troubles, where I am reminded of an especially terrible fortnight in 1988. On 6th March the IRA volunteers Daniel McCann, Seán Savage and Mairéad Farrell were shot by the SAS in Gibraltar. On the 16th, at their funeral in Milltown Cemetery, Belfast, the Loyalist Michael Stone, using a pistol and grenades, attacked the mourners, killing the IRA volunteer Caoimhín Mac Brádaigh (a.k.a. Kevin Brady) and two civilians, Thomas McErlean and John Murray. On the 19th, at Caoimhín Mac Brádaigh's funeral, two non-uniformed British Army corporals, David Howe and Derek Wood, were mistaken for Loyalist gunmen and attacked by civilians after driving their car into the funeral procession. The two were then shot dead by the IRA.

I have no memory and no way of knowing if these events shaped the poem. But their horrific mixture of intention and contingency reminds me how often death, back then, seemed a matter of taking the wrong turn on any given road; I'm reminded of the unreliability of maps. I write this a couple of weeks after the EU referendum of 23rd June 2016, when the British outpost of Gibraltar voted overwhelmingly to remain in Europe, and Britain voted to get out. I'm beginning to see how the poem might be seen in the light of those questions of identity and belonging, to which there are no clear answers. The figurative road map has yet to be drawn. I'm reminded of the last lines of the poem 'Belfast Confetti': "What is/ My name? Where am I coming from? Where am I going? A fusillade of question-marks."

PAUL CASEY

Exile

My mother is taking me to Africa
She takes me from the arms
of her mother, the reach
of her great-great-grandmothers

I breathe in the womb of Africa
and smile with African children
see their eyes reach through mine
to meet all my grandmothers.

'Exile' invites the reader into the dark heart of the unfamiliar, by way of simple imagery and language, to listen a moment inside its vastness and to rediscover there — the familiar. It questions openness and empathy and asks, at what point are we the same? How do we reconcile with loss, or embrace the solitude of being *other*? It is a song of being on the outside, using language from the inside, and vice versa. It calls to humanity's great need for cultural translation and inclusion. It's a poem of lament and of praise which celebrates and affirms that our earliest instinctual understanding is both naturally complex and uncompromisingly honest. It's a plea to distinguish individual experience from the shared and to recognise that we could all be in some form of personal exile. How many become estranged from an inherited or learned understanding during their lifetimes? Perhaps everyone. Perhaps often.

I have read and written poems that have violently washed me up into exile from my own sensibilities, or from what I had once believed in. Being true means allowing the important questions to be answered while accepting the risk of exile, which inevitably leads to rediscovery, clarity and true growth. This poem wants us to consider and embrace change and the foreign, to take the next crucial leap of courage. How often do people awaken to find themselves at a great distance from the very world they walk about in, from the world they know it *could* or *should* be? Perhaps few, I don't know. While writing or reading a poem is always both personal and political (which implies an element of self-imposed exile, however brief or permanent), it allows us to step outside the maze of the 'known' and to journey the untrodden, partly if not wholly on our own terms. And who knows, perhaps return laden yet again with the deliciously essential new.

PHILIP CASEY

Hamburg Woman's Song

Time has gone slowly by the hour,
by the year it has gone like a day
and you and I are of a sudden old.
But behind my bright eyes, papa,

I will always be a girl of ten,
and you, a grown man of twenty
when you cheated the dreaded police
who wanted to take me away.

I was born in a time and place
to a woman I look like now,
but fear grew like mould on bread
in my mother's love for her slow girl.

I remember the sirens and cobbles,
then waking at dawn by a stream
where you left me with a countrywoman
and time went slowly by the hour.

She who was my mother
died in the Hamburg fire,
and he who was my father
never came back from the east.

My hands hardened and my bones grew long.
I trusted what I could not understand
until one morning you came up the road
and happiness changed my face.

I am a woman of Hamburg
who walked to the hungry city
side by side with my new father.
I have lived here to this day.

S ometime in the mid-1980s, my friend Ulrike told me the
story of a remarkable woman and her adoptive father, and
brought me to meet the woman in Hamburg.

As a child from 1939 to 1945, she was in grave danger of being
murdered by the Nazis. An estimated 200,000 of the mentally
ill, the incurably ill, the physically or mentally handicapped,
and even the elderly were murdered under Hitler's eugenics
programme. Its victims were known as 'useless eaters.'

However, Ulrike's friend was lucky. At enormous risk,
a young communist smuggled her out of Hamburg to the
countryside, where a family looked after her.

Her parents did not survive the war, but her communist
saviour did, and once peace was declared he brought her to his
home where she was still living as his daughter when I met her.

I didn't meet her hero father, but their story made a deep
impression on me, and several months later I woke with the
complete poem in my head, as if it were a song.

In 2015, when Katie Donovan and Dermot Bolger organised
a reading in the Mansion House to celebrate my 65th birthday,
several of my family and friends read my poems. Ulrike read
'Hamburg Woman's Song', adding as an aside that it was the
only known record of the story.

I hope that in some small way it may serve as love's riposte to
the racists and neo-Nazis who again threaten the world.

SARAH CLANCY

Homecoming Queen

… in your humpy pine-lined hometown,
I am damaged goods, in the place
where you did your underage drinking
your voracious first-and-second cousin kissing
it seems I'm the inbred one —
and I'm not who you'd bargained on me being
when you planned this visit home,
you act like I have dyke emblazoned
on my forehead, even in the graveyard
you fear your grandparents will
resuscitate themselves and read it,
this makes you cruel, more concerned now
with pleasing people who are long past feeling
than with me standing here offended
but still alive and breathing …

… later in your neighbourhood bar
we meet your childhood friends
but I've grown clumsy then and lumpen
and you're humbled from having had
to come here with a gimp like me,
the friends are kind though they smile
and try to chat with your 'guest from Ireland'
but you see me through a critic's eyes
and to limit any further damage
or the possibility of me saying something gay
you answer every question for me …

… between rounds of darts and heartburn mojitos,
I use my few mis-accented words on the barman
but you only speak to me in English

and when I try to ease the tension
in my neck and shoulders and head outside
to join the smokers you mutter
'if you smoke that don't think
I'm going to kiss you'
and I don't need anything translated ...

... before I came here with you
being native played in my favour
though it's only now I know this,
in coming here you've got my measure
and it's smaller than we thought; less weighty,
in this faltering unsteady latitude
I stand to take my awkward turn at darts
and miss so badly even the bull's-eye mocks me
and I won't forgive you this because
it's the first time I've ever wanted to be different
and I won't forgive you for it ...

... later when you think I'm sleeping
I hear crying and it stops me breathing
for an instant until in the same way
that winter's slow freeze seeps in,
I feel scar tissue forming across the wasteland
of how we've hurt each other and it keeps spreading
until the grey thin light of early morning
when I climb down from my high horse
and despite myself I hold you
and despite yourself you want me to
and we go on with a few new wounds to tend to ...

I wrote this poem in Canada when I was there on a trip
to read poetry. Something in the muffled snowbound
landscape made me feel isolated and this poem is a not-

quite autobiographical attempt to examine what it feels like to feel out of place. Subject-wise though, the poem is more directly dealing with the problems that can emerge in any relationship when lovers try to bring their partners to the territory commonly known as 'home'. By home I don't just meant the house or family, I mean the culture, surroundings, relationships and the expectations that the place where we grow up exerts on us throughout our lives. This poem is dealing with a same-sex relationship too, though, and this, for people of my generation at least, adds another level of difficulty to the things that have to be navigated. In a same-sex relationship people like me who grew up in a very Catholic and anti-gay culture will all have had to come into their own adulthood and self-acceptance by making some sort of deal with themselves and the wider culture around them about how they will be perceived and how they will act and how they feel about themselves. Very often this journey has been one of physical exile and I think that is probably why I wrote this particular poem while I was away in another country. People like me have tended to leave the places we grew up in in order to have the space and freedom we needed to be ourselves. I think for many LGBT people, all of these issues add extra levels of difficulty to relationships; as well as the fraught and delicate business of trying to love each other we have to navigate how each person in the relationship came to terms with their own sexuality and its context, basically with how well we are able to love ourselves.

MICHAEL COADY

Assembling the Parts

Standing in sunshine
by Highway 84
I'm photographing a factory
which is no longer there

looking for my father
by an assembly line
that's halted
and vanished into air

catching the sepia ghost
of a young tubercular Irishman
who's left a rooming house
at 6 a.m. in a winter time
during the Depression

when my mother is still a girl
playing precocious violin,
a Miraculous Medal under
her blouse, in Protestant
oratorios in Waterford.

A pallid face in the crowd
in a dark winter time,
he's coughing in the cold,
assembling typewriters
in Hartford Connecticut,

waiting for blood on his pillow
to send him home, where he'll
meet her one ordinary

night with the band playing
'Solitude' in the Forester's Hall.

Fifty years on
he's nine Septembers dead
and a tourist in sunshine
by Highway 84
is photographing a factory
which is no longer there,

assembling the parts
of the mundane mystery,
the common enigma of journeys
and unscheduled destinations,

the lost intersections
of person and place and time
uniquely fathering everyman
out of the dark.

Albert Einstein is reputed to have said, "Coincidence is God's way of remaining anonymous". An engaging thought but who knows? People have wrestled with the knotty old questions of chance, fate and destiny for as long as the human race has been able to speculate on the enigma of life. How did it come about that two human beings who would beget a particular 'you' would somehow cross paths, with a resulting amorous entanglement leading to a new life? How, in the case of your parents, did that original meeting happen to happen?

In my case I know the story. The young man who would, out of the tangle of circumstance become my father, left Carrick-on-Suir for America when he was twenty. He was just in time for the Great Depression, but somehow found a job in a typewriter factory in Hartford, Connecticut. Conditions were harsh, but there were queues of hungry unemployed outside the gates waiting to take your place.

Meanwhile back in Ireland, a girl he'd not yet met was growing up in Waterford, training as a violinist and pianist of precocious talent. One night the young Irishman in America coughed himself awake to find blood on his pillow. He had the dreaded TB and was haemorrhaging.

Get back to Ireland, young man, was the Hartford's doctor's advice.

Years later in his cups he would dramatically describe the great storm the liner encountered on the passage back to Ireland.

One night he went to a dance in the local hall, chanced to meet the girl from Waterford who was playing piano with the band and fell in love to the tune of Duke Ellington's 'Solitude'. Six months later they married and I was born within a year.

Suppose he had never had that haemorrhage in Hartford, Connecticut? A lifetime later I found myself pulling in there on a Greyhound bus and, remembering my father's tracing, I went looking for the Underwood typewriter factory which was somehow entangled in my destiny.

That's what my poem 'Assembling the Parts' tells of. Most poems entail a process of recognition, for the writer first and then the reader. Call it epiphany if you like. And in the course of writing my poem I suddenly realised that the mundane timetable word 'destination' contains that deep word 'destiny', to the tune of Duke Ellington's 'Solitude'.

Metathesis

i

While she's waiting for the lights to change
at City Hall, the storm begins; the wind
speeds the river, lifts dust, yet traffic holds
her captive on the pavement. Pulsating
at the red-to-green, the seconds counted-
out, her body's dream-stuck lag behind her
ticking heels, the rush her heart's dictating
to the *slow, too slow* of other people,
she at last steps off the street. Descended
to the car park's underworld, on her knees
she tips her bag, finds keys, her ticket,
and becomes Persephone, reversing
fast into the dark — spinning on to where
she shouldn't go, but has to, doesn't care.

ii

She knows the story of Iris, rainbow
sent to a goddess with a god's request —
an order really, it occurs to her
on the platform, the station almost empty,
a gape in the bird-flecked, seascape roof now
holding those seven curved colours, the rest
of the sky pale beyond the glass. Easter
Monday passes, cold as Persephone
who craved the warmth of red, orange, yellow —
the green, blue, indigo, violet, fast-
dyed by the tears of her goddess-mother;
the ground beneath her quaking, she can't see
the train, still miles away, the ferrous dance
as track locks into track at its advance.

iii

Beyond the window's skin, a scattered white,
the many weathers March defines as light,
all that's left of the storm now its surface
of flotsam on the river she can't hear.
Up-tumbled desperately from mud, it's dragged
back to an underworld that's mapped and snagged
in the hollow of her cup. Silted there,
are tea-leaf letters that she tilts, re-shapes
to other orders, different words, the three
attempts to change what she, Persephone,
can only know — bare trees that never felt
the rip and snap until it was too late,
that never had the chance to turn about
in seasons she has made, can't live without.

'Metathesis' began with a word I either didn't know or had forgotten. Words are air to writers and it's possible I'd absorbed this word in much the same way one breathes through someone else's perfume in a crowd, or inhales a fug of over-roasted coffee beans while walking past a café. I may have parked it somewhere.

Poems are given to their makers in many ways, and, like most poets, I find it difficult to write 'about' a subject when challenged to do so. A poem has to offer me a way in and early drafts usually involve me looking for a door or even a window I can prise open. Poems are never given a pre-composition intellectual work-over.

All I had was a word, 'metathesis', and a feeling that keeping that word as a working title would affect the making or not making of the poem. I didn't look the word up in my dictionary, at least not until I had a grip on what I was trying to do. Images began to surface — vivid, cinematic, and so ephemeral that I was almost afraid to reach out for them. Looking back now at the first of many early drafts, I'm surprised at how many elements from those first scribbled pages in a notebook — the rushing river, the trees, the weather — have survived into the final version.

As a rule, I try to keep myself out of the act of composition as much as possible; any poem I've ever over-thought at the outset has ended up filed away in a drawer with a stake driven through its lifeless heart. I had no intentions for 'Metathesis' except to try and grab some of those images and take them to the page.

Stephen Spender wrote: "Poetry is a balancing of unconscious and conscious forces in the mind of the poet, the source of the poetry being the unconscious, the control being provided by the conscious." Examining those drafts now, I notice that I have numbered each hand-written line down to fourteen. This then is the point at which I must have started that balancing.

Catching a poem while it's still out of reach is always the most terrifying part of the process. Too light a touch and it's liable to get bogged down in abstraction, too heavy and it can be smothered. Once I move everything to the white screen, away from my handwriting, from my physical presence on the page and my imposition on the words, I pick up a trail and my instinct kicks in. That trail could be determined by the line breaks, the physical shape on the page, or by a single, 'concrete' image. It could be what I call the 'axle' word, the one around which the poem turns. It could be the rhyme, if there is one, or the form, again if there is one.

The British poet, Paul Farley has said that, 'Engaging with form — any form — means there's at least a chance that you'll say something you weren't going to say. Too much freedom gives you that rabbit-in-the-headlights thing.' This is something with which I concur (and repeat so often that I am in danger of having it inscribed on my headstone). Anne Sexton and Adrienne Rich have made similar comments. I've found that concentrating on the mechanics, so to speak, helps to take my mind away from any intentions I might have for long enough to allow the poem to come through. But I would write in form only if the poem demanded it.

As 'Metathesis' developed, I put the initial draft to one side. A second part was written; this rhymed, but with the end words set far apart, and an 'eye rhyme' towards the start, not loudly. What became the opening section of the triptych, unrhymed apart from the final couplet, came next. The initial draft I'd put aside ended up being the final part. I decided to experiment with rhyme patterns here to see what would happen. It surprised me by confirming 'Metathesis' as being the correct title for a poem concerned with the randomness of life — how a decision as seemingly quick and unfreighted with intent as simply moving one letter about in a word, for instance, can dictate the way in which a life is played out.

As for knowing when a poem is finished— well, I'm with Mr Yeats when he said that, "The correction of prose, because it has no fixed laws, is endless, a poem comes right with a click like a closing box." I tend to keep going until I hear (or at least think I can hear) that 'click.'

Even as part of a longer sequence, every poem has its own separate life while I'm working on it. Later, if it were to be placed between covers, I would hope that it should not only 'click' but talk to its neighbours. Like one of those vinyl records which, in pre-download days, we listened to all the way through from first track to last — albums written to be heard that way — a poem should be able to stand alone while keeping its place in the overall flow demanded by a book. The older I get, though, and the longer I'm writing, I'm finding that poems often arrive with their own unconsciously chosen place in that narrative already waiting.

But that's another discussion altogether.

Bench

I've always wanted a good table
there in the space by the window,
there where the sun comes crawling
in the morning.
The birds and the moon
could catch me working.

A cluttered table —
you can imagine it holding
books, papers, poems,
all kinds of scribbling —
an empty coffee cup,
the lamp burning long after midnight.

A sturdy table —
the kind the hero comes in
and lays his sword upon,
or the dead body of his son,
a table strong enough
to bear sorrow,
to bear fruit,
flowers from the field,
a feather dropped
through the open window.

A poet's table —
wide enough for the whiskey ballad,
long enough for the epic.
It must have a feel for sound.
The grain should run evenly,
a seam of gold that curves

and curves like a river of words
into the pool of a poem.

A good table —
I'd want the wood to be smooth,
pale as the undressed skin of a tree
so when the wind blows
over its bare back,
its soul will waken
to the memory of leaves and forest.

A useful table —
not a perfect table.
If it is chipped or scratched
it will remind me
of rooks and cuckoo
fox and squirrel.
But I want nothing broken,
nothing that speaks
of the axe, the chisel, or the saw.

When I come to the table
in the morning, I want to feel
like a woodsman hunting
or in the evening, a nesting bird.
What I want is to be lost
in the forest of myself.

Though I've searched for years
I've never found such a table
nor the carpenter to make it.
All I have is this: hear how it creaks.

The first poem I wrote after my father died was 'Bench'. It is the only poem of mine that won't stay in my head, but I think I know the reason why. My father was a brass-finisher with J&C McLoughlin's of Pearse Street. The firm used to trade just across from the old redbrick library.

He made church furniture, anything in brass, bronze, gold and silver. My father was a great man for prayer and believed in hard work. His brothers were Cistercian monks; he himself was a quiet man who could tell a great yarn. And like the man in Frost's poem 'Mending Wall', he liked the old sayings: "Good fences make good neighbours"; "If a thing is worth doing, it is worth doing well".

I was an odd child, wonky in more ways than was possible. I was never good at school, hopeless until I got to university. I liked songs more than prayers, bands more than church. I hadn't a plan, so neither he nor I had any idea what I was doing with my life.

As he got older and I straightened out, we mellowed. 'Bench' comes from a day I called in to see him. He was in his shed, mending or making something. I told him I had bought a bench. He took my hands in his and said, "These soft hands are only good for one thing. I have a bench; a desk is what you have."

So perhaps the correct title for this poem should be 'Desk', but the poem is all about my father, my writing, and me; so 'Bench' it is.

PÁDRAIG J. DALY

Complaint

I will tell you, Sir, about a woman of yours,
Who suddenly had all her trust removed
And turned to the wall and died.

I remember how she would sing of your love,
Rejoice in your tiniest favour:
The scented jonquils,

The flowering currant bush,
The wet clay
Spoke to her unerringly of benevolence.

I remind you, Sir, of how, brought low,
She cowered like a tinker's dog,
Her hope gone, her skin loose around her bones.

Where were you, Sir, when she called out to you?
And where was the love that height nor depth
Nor any mortal thing can overcome?

Does it please you, Sir, that your people's voice
Is the voice of the hare torn between the hounds?

'Complaint' came about like this. I had a friend called
Monica. She was warm, generous, full of laughter.
She visited the sick and housebound. She tended an
amazing garden, filled with fruit, vegetables, *samhaircíní* and
scented stock. She made delicious biscuits.

But she fell ill. Her illness brought on deep depression. The
last time I visited her — a day or two before she died — she had

no interest in speaking to me or to anybody. She turned away from me to the wall.

As a priest, I had attended many people in their last moments. I watched as they slipped quietly into God. Monica's death was different. There was nothing sweet or peaceful about it. For several months afterwards I found it hard to pray, not realising that this had any connection to Monica. A good director on a retreat got to the crux of things straight away. She traced my prayer difficulties back to my disappointment with God about Monica. She encouraged me to follow the example of Jeremiah in the Old Testament and express my annoyance. "Pray as you are, not as you think you ought to be". My prayer became a poem.

I was not conscious, when I was writing, that I was echoing Hopkins in addressing God disdainfully as 'Sir'.

KATHY D'ARCY

Probable Misuse of Shamanism

I clamber through your Great Vein
(or Inferior Vena Cava,
as it is properly known).
Surrounded by black, stagnant blood, and
the beat of the drum, if I work
hard enough I will come
to the writhing bowl of your Right Atrium,
and then the possibilities are endless.

I can sit quite still, with choking gutful
of irony wine, and allow
my foreign-ness to disrupt the smooth flow
(Turbulence, that is called)
through the Mitral Valve, so that
little clots form and are shot around and out
to your lungs;
an exercise in anticipation for me, the knowing wait
for the sharp pain, the breathless death.

I can kick and claw at the great central wall
to make a small hole, and squeeze through
to the business side; from there
I will have no choice
But to be shunted straight to your brain,
whence a dullness will spread
and the 'F-A-S-T' protocol from the stroke ads
will come into play.
Then, like that old film, I will have to exit through
the nearest opening (your rheumy eye probably) before
I run out of 'T for Time'.

I can simply tear it apart —
though this would be most difficult, it feels
the most satisfying —
begin with cutting the beautiful strings,
then rip off the valve-lips like so many yoghurt lids,
finally work my hands bloody
(like crying in a swimming pool)
taking the central divide asunder;
yes, how satisfying to gut it like that, so
nothing can hide!

Sometimes I feel so much strength
that I think I could reach in under
your straining ribcage with my bare hand
and pluck the grotesque, pulsating thing out
like a weed;
but they beat independently, and
I cant imagine not flinging it away in disgust,
not screaming and stamping like a child with
an eel, not cowering in a corner while
the pathetic lump convulses its last.

The book says to make sure and come out
before the drum-beat stops;
I'm not sure what happens otherwise.

Probably *Misuse* ... is one of my most-read poems for many
reasons, and the first of these is that I read it standing
on one leg, with one eye closed and one arm extended,
my index finger pointed straight ahead. I've done this hundreds
of times now, and the curse has still not come true. I've never
actually done it in the presence of the intended accursed; maybe
I don't genuinely want it to work. Still, a disappointing result for
someone inspired by the great *filí*, ancient Irish poets second

only to royalty whose curses, delivered as aforementioned, actually did work and were greatly to be feared.

It isn't that cursing and vengeance are mainstays of my practice, more that I believe in the power of poetry to bring about real — maybe magical — change where violence and polemic fail. In 2013 I performed my play *This is My Constitution* for a Dáil Éireann briefing of TDs and Senators as part of the Constitutional Convention on Gender. I write poems that address human rights abuses still perpetrated in Ireland, from direct provision conditions to anti-choice legislation. I don't plan to do this (I didn't plan the curse) but when I read in public I see how creativity can spark discussion and break down polarisations. I'm now using a PhD to investigate the possible use of poetry instead of academic forms to transmit knowledge (essentially what the *filí* used it for).

Sometimes, of course, a good curse is called for: anatomy, and particularly that of the heart, was always going to be my register of choice in those instances. I trained as a doctor, and will never lose my fascination with that imperial organ, which, according to the sixteenth-century physician William Harvey, 'beats of itself, and does not stop unless for ever'. There is much poetry in a human heart — not, I'm at pains to point out, the romanticised cypher, but the fleshy misshapen knob of muscle which is almost like a parasite in our chests. I used to think I would have to reach in through people's ribs and grasp the fussy little creatures if I was ever to truly connect with anyone (a kind of gruesome Golden Goose myth). My poetry has grown softer since then: I have learned to curse less, to let hearts lie in their dark nests, to take humans at face value. For now.

MICHAEL DAVITT

Déirc

do Mhoira

Níor leor na silíní fiáine chun ár sciúch a fhliuchadh tar éis
   uair an chloig
de shiúlóid i mbeirfean an mheán lae. Bhí braoinín uisce uainn
   go géar.

Seana-bhean de dhéine shéimh Pheig Sayers
fé chruitín údarásach a d'oscail doras ársa an tí feirme Gasconne.

An mbeadh *un verre d'eau* aici? Bheadh agus bucaod!
is d'iompaigh sí láithreach uainn i dtreo fhionnuaire chrón na
   cistine.

An mar seo a bhí le déircínteacht fadó? Gan aon éileamh mór
   a dhéanamh
ach a bheith i láthair in am an ghátair agus an chruinne ag
   athroinnt a coda?

Ar nós an tseana-fhráma rothair leis an leathroth búclálta
a bhronn m'athair ar an dtincéir mná mar aon le púnt siúicre,

is chuimhníos im gharsún gurb shin an fáth go mbíonn seana-
   fhrámaí rothair ann
is gurbh shin an chiall go ndeintear rothaí a bhúcláil.

D'fhill bean an uisce gan mhoill le crúiscín lán na déirce agus
   dhá ghloine
á rá go mbeadh a thuilleadh is a thuilleadh ann dúinn dá mba
   ghá.

Agus fíon fuar an tobair bheannaithe ag beannú ár scornacha
sheas ár seana-bhean i mbéal an dorais —

a haoibh roicneach ag lonrú as an scáil
fé mar gu'b'i féin a bhí ag fáil na déirce ón mbeirt thincéir.

Lahas, 16/06/05

Alms

for Moira

The wild cherries weren't enough to slake our throats after an
    hour
of walking in the sweltering heat of midday. We badly needed
    a drop of water.

An old woman of Peig Sayer's gentle severity
under a commanding hunch opened the door of the Gascony
    farmhouse.

Would she have a glass of water? Yes and a bucketful!
and she turned from us instantly into the dark yellow coolness
    of the kitchen.

Was this how it was begging alms long ago? Not to make a
    huge demand
but to be present at the time of want and the universe handing
    out her portions.

Like the bicycle frame with the buckled wheel
which my father gave to the tinker woman with a pound of sugar.

I thought as a boy that was why the old frames were there
and that was the reason the wheels were buckled.

The woman of the water returned without delay with a jug full
     of alms and two glasses
saying that there was more and more still for us if needed.

And as the blessed cold wine of the sacred well blessed our throats
our old woman stood in the doorway

her wrinkly smile shining out of the shadows
as if she herself was receiving the alms from the two tinkers.

On Thursday the 16th of June 1995 Michael came into our bedroom early in the morning and gave me a gift of a new poem, 'Déirc'. It was inspired by a hike we had just made through the gentle Gascon countryside of our home in Lahas, France.

Michael was very excited at the time because he felt that poems were flowing through him freely. I cherish the poem because it was the last one Michael completed.

It remains a gift to have his astute take on a shared moment. I love the way he bridges the world of rural Gascony with the Cork of his childhood, the way an old French farmer could just as easily be a Blasket woman.

There were recurring themes in *Seimeing Soir,* the collection which Michael had published just six months previously. The great wide, open blue skies of the south west of France afforded Michael the time and space to reflect on the journey from young lover in the Gaeltacht to older somewhat bruised wiser man. His humour remained intact, his compassion had deepened.

To me 'Déirc' is perfectly balanced. Having asked for so little, we were blessed by the water we were given. And yet the supply was endless.

I can remember when Michael read the poem to me that morning. I felt blessed to be constantly enriched by his passion for our spiritual and cultural heritage. We are all the richer that he shared it so beautifully, defiantly, sharply and wittily with us.

— **Moira Sweeney**

GERALD DAWE

The Water Table

for Tom & Julie Kilroy

The house is floating on water —
rain-water, seepage off fields,
rivers, thaw, the eventual sea.
Maybe we're all floating.

The house moored like a boat
in this one particular place,
sways through days and nights
when we're glued to the TV.

The water table's rising.
Soon typewriter and microwave,
chairs, teapots, family-pictures
will float up into the trees

and come to rest, like offerings
around a holy well, glistening.
Already I have seen the ground swell
and foundation cracks settle.

Sometime in the 1980s, when we lived in Corrandulla in County Galway, there was one particularly bad summer, not unlike recent times indeed. The rain started falling quite early in the morning as we drove into town to collect our son and a friend who was going to stay over. It was obvious we were in for a soaking as we headed down the Curragh Line into town. Lough Corrib, which we normally could barely see, was distinctly there in the distance and the various local rivers that fed into and from it were beginning to reach the same level as the road. By the time we were returning from Galway parts of the road were under water, the old bridges over the smaller rivers could not withstand the flow and were becoming unpassable and as we turned into the front yard of the house signs were indeed ominous. The rain could no longer run off into gutters and drains dug at the roadside. It was a ceaseless deluge and by early afternoon rain was entering the house itself. By nightfall we had been flooded. As a result of that estranging and costly experience that led to a JCB excavating a huge soakage pit in the garden (and solved the problem should it ever recur), I started to read a lot about water and its earthly pathways. I was fascinated how hydrology — engineering the flow and patterns of rain, river and sea tidally connect (or not as the case may be) — is a very poetic concept. It also occurred to me that notwithstanding all our human desire for permanency and residence, nature has very much its own rhythm and necessities that takes absolutely no account of our being there. Around the same time I was very interested in the Russian artist Marc Chagall and had several books with his wondrously coloured topsy-turvy village-world. So between one thing and another everything gelled into 'The Water Table', a poem about transience and how fluid the imagined world really is, no matter how hard we pretend to think that everything is knowable and definitive. Even the phrase seemed to me to capture the unpredictability of what happens when you sit down to make a poem: the water table.

JOHN F. DEANE

The Poem of the Goldfinch

Write, came the persistent whisperings, a poem
on the mendacities of war. So I found shade
under the humming eucalyptus, and sat,
patienting. Thistle-seeds blew about on a soft breeze,
a brown-gold butterfly was shivering on a fallen
ripe-flesh plum. Write your dream, said Love, of the total
abolition of war. Vivaldi, I wrote, the four
seasons. Silence, a while, save for the goldfinch
swittering in the high branches, *sweet*, they sounded,
sweet-wit, wit-wit, wit-sweet. I breathed
scarcely, listening. Love bade me write but my hand
held over the paper; tell them you, I said,
they will not hear me. A goldfinch swooped,
sifting for seeds; I revelled in its colouring, such
scarlets and yellows, such tawny, a patterning
the creator himself must have envisioned, doodling
that gold-flash and Hopkins-feathered loveliness. Please
write, Love said, though less insistently. Spirit, I answered,
that moved out once on chaos ... No, said Love,
and I said Michelangelo, Van Gogh. No, write
for them the poem of the goldfinch and the whole
earth singing, so I set myself down to the task.

I have always loved the short and quietly dramatic poem by
George Herbert, 'Love': it begins

Love bade me welcome
But my soul drew back, guilty of dust and sin.

72

The drama unfolds as the soul, conscious of its unworthiness, is gently cajoled into coming in, sitting down, and being served. The host is 'Love' which is, in Herbert's mind, God, but may be whatever higher power one believes in. This poem is an echo behind my own piece which was thrust upon me as a form of gift, or grace, one day as I sat under a eucalyptus tree which seemed to be humming with bees and flies that feasted on its leaves and flowers. When a flock of goldfinch settled nearby on thistle-heads and on the seeds forming on the tree, I was stunned once more by the beauty that our world offers. When I wrote that poem, as now, wars were rife and I wondered what a lyric poet might do to help; it seemed that such work, in a quiet part of Ireland, had nothing to do with the great movements of history. Herbert's poem suggested that whatever a writer might do, he/she should always try to do better, thus adding to the scales of justice, and of good and evil, something of value that might, in however small a way, help to tilt the balance in favour of the good. So, all work undertaken with integrity and effort may add to the sum of human worth. The poem came, and with it the sense that I must value poetry for its own sake, and work as I possibly could. This poem, then, celebrates the beauty of our earth, and celebrates the value of poetry itself, and set me on a path of study and work that my own lyric efforts might be of the best.

MARY DORCEY

Trying On For Size

Capsized on the bed you roll, cane white
legs treading the air. You are pulling on
your stockings, easier now this way than to
stand upright and bend. You are laughing
because I've caught you at it, one of your
secret stratagems. On the beach in summer,

Years ago, when you were young, in august,
a careless hero for an hour, your limbs
long and full, shoulders broad, intent on
freedom, land and charges cast of, you
swam with mighty strokes out so far, we
watched in awe until your beauty was a

Bird or buoy dancing between waves. With
each new day behind us, do you remember
when, you ask. And, I do, almost all of it
and more. You were not in all moods good.
You threatened with a wooden spoon —
cursed me when there was no one else

To curse. Moored in a kitchen that over-
heard wild ocean you did not always
counsel or console. How often did your
gaze flinch from trouble, having known
too well the weight of grief uncomforted?
But you had a window looking south, books

To read by evening light, a work-store of
song. You named these one by one as grace
and stood them against storm. Going down

the stairs in present days, our shoes fitted
to your infant, halting gait, I want to pick
you up and carry you or launch you across

The bannister as you did me, in this house
where we played, making up childhood
together. But the time has run out or arrived.
Now you must take every step first along
this passage. We daughters follow after,
each one moving into the space cleared by

Our mothers. And with what fine nerve, what
unthanked poise, you confront this last world
you will discover before me. I catch your shy,
jaunty smile at the mirror: see you say —
what do you think? As if death were a foolish,
extravagant hat you were trying on for size.

This poem gave its name to my second collection, *Moving into the Space Cleared by Our Mothers*. It came to me in the last lines one day long before I had become interested in the experience as a subject for writing. The daughter is looking after her mother following an illness. For the first time the daughter sees her as vulnerable and in need. The daughter remembers her childhood when these roles were reversed. It arrived as a kind of premonition of what was to come much later. It sounded the first note in a series about the mother/daughter relationship, the shape-shifting roles between a child and ageing parent, when the daughter finds herself becoming the parent and returning love and care in the manner and kind she once received it. I was struck by and wanted to reveal the fluidity and complexity of this relationship where two individuals conflict, reflect and care for each other throughout life. A subject still not often represented in literature.

I grew up in a house by the sea almost close enough to jump into it from my bedroom window.

My mother was widowed when I was seven and my eldest brother sixteen. This sorrow marked us all. But we had many compensations. Firstly my mother's strength, secondly that we lived in a household full of books, and that both our parents encouraged imagination.

As soon as I learned to read I began to write; the desire came as early as my love of animals and the sea. I made up poems on my way to primary school and turned up late for class because I was finishing a story. But becoming a 'writer' was another thing entirely. Growing up in the Ireland of the 1960s it seemed clear that most of our artists lived in exile and the few women writers in print at the time were upper class and independently wealthy. I saw no way that a girl like me could be a professional writer. And, after all, I had read enough of the great literature of Europe and America to know that the world had no pressing need for any more novels or stories.

It took my involvement in the women's movement in the 1980s to persuade me that a great void existed that I had failed to see until then: the comparative absence of writing by women about the lives of women. With a few radiant exceptions, men wrote most of the 'great books' that dealt with women. I began to see that the reality of life as lived by women and the daily facts of our existence had been written out of history. And like many others at this period I realised that if I wanted to read the kind of books that would speak to me about my life I would have to write them myself.

I could say my journey as a writer has been defined by a desire to explore and reveal 'otherness', the way in which societies create castes of insider and outsider. Many accounts of 'otherness', whether of sexual orientation, gender, race or age, are corralled in a kind of quarantine, separated from so-called 'normal' society. When I write about erotic/romantic same-sex relationships or political oppression or old age I want to place my so-called outsiders where they belong — within the mainstream of human experience. I try to write in the most naked and undefended language I can find so that the reader is drawn right into the heart of the emotion, and jolted from their usual safe seat of detachment.

And the truth, of course, is that we all play many different roles throughout our lives, insiders in one group, outsiders in another. And we will all become outsiders when we age.

Even if we lived in a world of total equality and inclusion I would still want to write because the process of matching sound to sense, idea to image, memory to present, is the most fulfilling endeavour I know, and one of the best ways of being human.

Nine books later I am still doing what I love most, every day searching for new directions and hoping to find in the choice and ordering of words a channel to reach a deeper level of truth.

THEO DORGAN

On a Day Far From Now

Death will come and have your eyes
and I will go into her arms
without fear or hesitation.

Frost on the slates
of our beloved square,
the cars riding low under
a hurrying sky when

I open the great hall door
and take her hand,
her long black coat.

The bare-flagged hallway, frost
and perfume on the night air.

I watch her let down
her gleaming hair,
open her slender arms
in your exact gesture.

Death will come and have your eyes
and I will go into her arms
alone and unafraid.

after a line by Cesare Pavese

I remember exactly the moment this poem was born. I was In Annaghmakerrig working with a group of Irish poets, team-translating two Greek poets. As you walk into the kitchen from the drawing room where we'd been working there's a double set of doors and a step down. Someone had just quoted a line from Cesare Pavese, "Death will come and have your eyes" and, struck by the double meaning — Death will pluck out your eyes, Death's eyes will be your eyes — I was distracted for a moment and almost fell down the step. The jerk, the recovery of balance, the ambiguous phrase, all tumbled together in a split-second flash of light: I saw the poem, or at least the kernel of the poem, as if in the air before me. It might be as helpful to say I tasted the opening lines in my mouth, heard them out beyond me or felt them as a pressure in the air around me.

> *Death will come and have your eyes*
> *and I will go into her arms …*

At the time I was living in Dublin's Merrion Square, and the high entrance hall flashed before me, with its heavy front door, its flagged, scrubbed floor. Then I could see the door opening, hear the low hum of traffic, see the railings across the road … but (and I'd walked outside now, past the pond by the back door, out into Bernard Loughlin's crafted garden), what of the 'you' implied in "your"? My beloved's eyes, of course, and her arms. Death as the beloved, returning for me … I remember a feeling of buoyancy, of being borne up on the thought-image, on the notion that there would be, after all, life for these lovers after the dark of passing from this world. That there would be no separation. I had the whole first draft before the kettle inside had boiled.

CAL DOYLE

Sirens

SUGGESTIVE SEA OF FLAME

Dear Sir: please feel free to devour me
like you would a cupcake, or a kebab
with many trimmings. My nation is trapped
in its womb of conflict:
the sun is blackened by the souls of
our slain young men. Do you like my pictures?
I am naked just for you, prospective husband
six hundred and eleven. The moon is abundant
in its punishment. All tides have stopped,
that is, except the tide of my sex [winking emoticon]
which will drown our genitals before dawn.

GRACEFUL MACHINE

My feet are exquisite: I very much need you
to nuzzle them with your handsome features
or baptise them in a bowl filled
with multi-coloured confections, like Skittles
or M&Ms. My hometown is a maze.
We have a fortune-teller who smells like the rain.
He cupped my naked breasts when I
was fourteen, and told me that my father
was his lover. Eat the sweets from in between my toes.
Be fluid. Later I will eat you. Do not pause.
Keep eating. It doesn't matter that I weep.

You will find my torso to your pleasure.
I am the source of all seafarers' most vigorous
erections since *One Thousand and One Nights*
and my scales are electronic: please open the link. I wish
for you to see the currents of electricity
disarrange and multiply my erotic centre: not the 'gem'
that you seek, hooded, hidden beneath the labia, but every
scale: I can't swim in a straight line because of them.
Strum me like a guitar: my ecstatic spasms have killed men
larger than you. I have smashed through ceilings
and broken every brittle bone in my body.

Sometimes 'Sirens' bothers me, sometimes I'd rather that it didn't exist, other times I think it aspires to reveal the discrepancies between words and what they try to mean, and that's what all half-decent poems should at least attempt to look at. Although it reads as if assembled and collaged, the text is all original; there are no 'found' elements outside of the titles (which are strange little objects in themselves). If you'll indulge my butchering of a quote from Fredric Jameson: pastiche is parody without the humour. I've always found that to be a terrifying and tremendously useful concept.

Before I sent this poem out to any journals, I ran it by three or four female poet-friends for their opinion. *Please be brutal. This is plainly vile stuff. Why did I produce this?* Reports back were positive. *Go with it. The voices are genderless. Japonica. Feminist. Anti-capitalist.* So I sent it out & it found a home with a few other poems of mine in *The Stinging Fly*, which was a welcome surprise. But it still feels like problematic work to me. As a series of unheimlich sonnets, both in shape and pitch, it is successful, more or less. But whenever I read it publicly it I want to disown it. Whenever I go back over it in private, it strikes an uneasy spark in me. Writing it felt like painting something: the words felt material, the meaning felt secondary. It reads to me now like this old dark song, one I desperately wish to escape, but deep inside there lies the sonic skeleton upon which everything I attempt to scribble is hung.

MARTINA EVANS

The Day My Cat Spoke to Me

for Geraldine More O'Farrell

I was surprised not so much by the fact
that she spoke
but by the high opinion she had of me.
'I think you're great,' she said
and it was at this point I looked at her
in surprise.
'I mean,' she continued, 'the way
you've managed to write anything at all!
Fourteen court hearings
and that horrible barrister,
the way she looked at you.'
'But you weren't there,' I said.
'Oh but I can imagine it,' said Eileen,
her yellow eyes opening wide
before narrowing into benevolent slits.
'I only had to look at you,
gulping down your red lentil soup
when you came home after nearly three
hours in the witness box defending
your right to write.
Did anyone ever hear the like?
I could see it all in every swallow you took,
her butty legs and her manly shoulders
in that black suit, did she have dandruff?
I hope not, because it really shows up on black.
Saying those things to you,
Oh Miss Cotter we would all like the luxury
of sitting at home writing books!
Holding up paper evidence between finger

and thumb *Here is another job*
you failed to get Miss Cotter.
Trying to make you go out to work
with radiation in a hospital
and who would take care of us?
What would the cats of this house
do without the sound of your pen scratching
on paper, the hum of your computer,
your lovely lap and the sound of you
on the telephone?
The big dyed blonde head of her!
And where did she think she was going?
Well, earning a lot of money for her own words
by the looks of things.
And saying them to you!
The best writer that ever heaved a can of Tuna
or opened a pack of Science Plan.
And as Mary Jenkins said about him
who paid for the horrible utterances,
It's just as well that Shakespeare wasn't married to him.
And then when he was in the witness box, he wished
you the best of luck with your writing ....'
At this point Eileen paused, closed her eyes.
I was waiting for her to say something witty herself.
After all it was a great opportunity for irony
which for some reason I have
always associated with cats.
But when she opened her eyes again
she requested a scoop of softened butter
after which she licked her lips in detail
and hasn't opened her mouth since
if you don't count yawning, lapping,
eating, washing, miaowing,
and screeching at intruders.

Poems beget other poems although the lineage is often murky as poems take their time to emerge, mulching down in the back brain. It's hard to say exactly where they come from, but not this poem, which stands out — not only because the main source is clear but also because it marked my return from prose to poetry.

I brought Frank O'Hara's 'True Account of Talking to the Sun on Fire Island' to my creative writing class for the students use as a model. The O'Hara poem is itself a response to Mayakovsky's 'An Extraordinary Adventure Which Befell Vladimir Mayakovsky in a Summer Cottage' and I was urging them to be playful, not to be afraid to be absurd or to praise their own work. This was the one exercise that stumped them. Disappointed, on the bus home I found myself scribbling on my folder, following my own instructions. It seemed that I was the one who needed the writing exercise. The constant harassment of a legal case was strangling my novel-in-progress despite all my efforts to push through. To turn to poetry was a gigantic psychic relief. This was a way to tell the truth 'slant' as Emily Dickenson urges us to do. I was exhausted in Dante's dark wood in the middle of my life, controlled every way I turned, and it was unbearable. Careful reasoning and totting up the sum saved by avoiding childcare fees satisfied the judge, but I was the cat who had enough of her tail being pulled. I did not need an image of anything great like the sun or even Czesław Miłosz's poetry tiger lashing his tail. A domestic cat would do. The words emerged in one long relieved hiss and, with the poem, the realisation that the kind of fiction I was being asked to write had become like the law to me, about money and rules. Poetry was outside of that, truly subversive. I've stayed with it since.

JOHN FITZGERALD

The Collectors

While she slept on, he would gather up
the bursts of birdsong around her window,
hiss-cracks of whipbird coming down
from the rainforest, a morning star as
one by one they all pulled out
to follow the bright space-station of their dreams.

During the day, there'd be eucalypts standing
like beasts of burden in the solid heat,
the tremor he felt when she'd say the word *creek*,
lorikeets rocketing through street trees, and
once, the draw and sigh of evening sea
as she pressed close to him, whispering a dream
of the leaf-thin tail of an eel tonguing its way
through the rocks of the waterfall pool.

Later, he'd empty his pockets,
adding to the prize shells, seed-pods, found
stones in her basket on the bookstand,
and wait for when she might take it down,
carry it out to the veranda, tip everything
across the sandy table-top
and examine each piece carefully,
her face glowing in amber candlelight, then
replace them all slowly, one by one,
her own particular way.

Place is by definition unavoidable, unless one dwells wholly
in spirit — which is possible. Places exert influence:
attracting, holding, repelling. A place can also inure and,

even while physically apparent, be completely absent from one's consciousness. Writers have a fine-tuned sense of place, often relating to their places in ways as complex and fulfilling as with the people of their lives. One thinks of Graves and Deia, Heaney and Mossbawn, Thompson and Woodbrook, Larkin and … everywhere.

In being asked to chose a poem that is representative, I feel a bit of a phoney, mainly because I've not yet published much of my work and so, in the absence of any wider exposure beyond intersecting circlets of friends and fellow writer-readers, must have a dangerously internalised sense of what 'representative' might mean. And yet, despite this reservation — itself a state of refuge — I have the freedom from imposed label and expectation to follow the creative instinct experimentally across a variety of forms, subjects and treatments.

The poem I have selected comes out of a conflicted frequent desire to get away from the familiarity of my life, as represented at one level by place as home, and to travel. To travel not for the journeying, which is more of a process of de- and re-compression, but in order to be in the new place and experience the difference, distance and alienation that such displacement brings. And by doing so, enter a state of intimacy which is rarefied by that sense of heightened experience that comes from being somewhere new or different to the ordinary. And then the parlour games begin: of how that place relates to the others of my life; how its creeping familiarity confounds the aim in travelling there in the first place; how the ties of blood and love exert and manifest in elected isolation. And how all of these doubts and questions and clarities surface and enter colloquy to emerge inevitably like postcards or dispatch notes in my case as poems.

GABRIEL FITZMAURICE

Dad

A man before his time, he cooked and sewed,
Took care of me and Mammy in her bed,
Stayed in by night and never hit the road.
I remember well the morning she was dead
(I'd been living up in Arklow — my first job
I hit the road in patches coming home),
He came down from the room, began to sob,
'Oh Gabriel, Gabriel, Gabriel, Mam is gone.'
He held me and I told him not to cry
(I loved her too, but thought this not the place —
I went up to her room, cried softly 'Why'
Then touched her head quite softly, no embrace)
Now when the New Man poses with his kid,
I think of all the things my father did.

I don't really have a favourite poem of mine. As I grow older
some of my erstwhile favourites have ceased to engage me.
A number still do. Poems I might take to the grave with me.
    One such poem is 'Dad', a sonnet. I like formal verse when
it works. And 'Dad' not only works for me, it has a profound
effect on audiences when I perform it at readings. It touches
people, makes them cry.
    My mother had rheumatic fever as a child. It damaged her
heart. She was a semi-invalid from my early years. Then she
had an operation to expand the mitral valve in her heart.
    That gave her a few short years of good health until the valve
contracted again.
    My father, a small farmer's son who had returned to his
native Moyvane from factory work in England during the
Second World War, met and married my mother, also a

Moyvane native, about 1950. I was born in 1952. From the early 60s my father was running our little grocery shop alone as my mother was confined to the chair and to the bed.

Not only did he run the shop, he ran the house as well; he cleaned he cooked he sewed he gardened he took care of Mam and me.

I was moved to write 'Dad' some years before he died. One Sunday I read in the paper about the New Man, a man who could push a pram and change a nappy. You'd swear it was rocket science. I thought about my father who had done so much before it was popular or profitable. And here were these celebrities posing in every sense of the word for the cameras.

I wrote the poem for my father. I'm glad I did it while he was still alive. He deserved to know how much I loved him.

ANNE-MARIE FYFE

The Red Aeroplane

From the oratory window I witness
mid-air doom, a slew of concentric
swirls, a trail of forge-sparks,
and that's it. A vermilion two-seater
stagger-wing loops earthbound,
so much depending upon centrifugal
drive. Slivers of toughened glass
spangle the outer stone sill,
the vacant co-pilot seat
is plummeted deep in rosebed mulch.

I question now if the red bi-plane
ever was, the way sureties tilt
and untangle from any one freezeframe
to its sequel. Maybe I was glimpsing
that two-seater red pedal car
— injection-moulded plastic —
collected one Christmas Eve night
for a fevered child? Or conflating
the replica cherry-red sixty-three
we'd toyed with, tinkered with, briefly
on a tinsmith's covered stall
that drenched Saturday?
                            What can't be
cast in any doubt is the wreckage,
a fragmentary scattering,
the mangledness on the far side
of glass. And how a Galway blue
skyscape proves ineluctably
the exponential function of tangents.

I t's been a late night in Galway (putting the world to rights with another poetry reading) and early-morning Atlantic rain is sheeting down on the Saturday Farmer's Market. The only half-sane option is to huddle under the nearest stall's tarpaulin, with no intention of buying, but — and here's the serendipity — suddenly this one's a Geppetto's cave, a whirr of clockwork, a toymaker's with the most exact, handmade retro cars, not from my children's time, but from way back before plastic, when toys were all enamelled tin.

To feign interest I fiddle with the tiny clockwork handle on a perfect miniature cherry-red enamel sports car and I'm at once drivin' on down to New Orleans with Chuck Berry, and at the same time, less exuberantly, back home in Cushendall where I'm collecting a red moulded-plastic pedal car my father's ordered from the general store for his first grandchild's first family Christmas, one that had its own worries and stresses.

And just as suddenly again I'm lifting off in a red stagger-wing plane that belongs to an Emmylou Harris song, past churches and steeples and railings and convent windows (perhaps that's how I see Galway, or all of home, as an endless mirrored replication of my own convent school with its gardeners and grottoes and manicured rosebeds) into some futuristic stratosphere where past is present, and flight is now, and toys and reality are indistinguishable, and anything is probable, everything is possible.

Except, as in so many of my poems since 2001, the limitless world of flight, the escape from the everyday, from the dragging-down rain and clerical greyness, there's an unequal mix of doom and jubilation, an uneasy cocktail of disaster and excitement. A mathematician friend still wants me to explain how a skyscape could prove 'ineluctably / the exponential function of tangents' but physics, too, is just part of the hyperreality that takes over in the single, concentric moment where the whole of life swirls around one small perfect bittersweet thing.

91

MATTHEW GEDEN

Photosynthesis

How plantlike we've become.
Your finger fronds limp from days of rain
curl around the steering-wheel. A low
pressure rests on our shoulders, the tension
of being kept in the dark too long. We
sway like half-drunk poppies. The car lurches

through stony silence. At the shore
we stop in the grey mist, your lips the only
colour for miles. Yet suddenly there is
a glimmer. The gloom recedes and figures
come out of the haze. The sea becomes
a white-haired Turner throwing light upon

our predicament. Even my predilection for
definition is surprised by the sudden edge
and the realisation that everything we see
is luminance. Out of the car I straighten up.
Reaching for warmth I part the clouds,
soak up sunlight and begin to breathe

more easily. You are there beside me.
We breathe together noticing shades
and textures as if for the first time.
Your eyes are many colours. Re-energised
we share complexities. We nourish each
other and scatter our hopes to the wind.

I am envious of poets such as the late Miroslav Holub who was able to draw upon a vast knowledge of the scientific world. Excellence in the sciences eluded me at school; I scraped a Physics 'O' Level and failed so miserably in a Chemistry multiple-choice paper that the teacher gleefully pointed out that a monkey with a pen would in all probability have scored higher. Nevertheless, a basic superficial interest remains and 'Photosynthesis' arose directly out of that.

I had been reading about the process whereby plants are able to convert light into chemical energy which then helps to sustain them. It occurred to me that our own need for sunlight affected our own growth and development and the poem began to move from there. That summer had been a particularly poor one in Ireland and the seemingly endless days of 'soft' drizzle soon lost any charm they might once have had. I was thinking of seasonal affective disorder, SAD, which had only relatively recently been identified and thought of how it must not only affect individuals but also relationships. The couple in the poem are travelling in "stony silence" and there is a tension both inside and outside the car which is only lifted by the glimmer of sunlight and the parting of the clouds.

'Photosynthesis' is not just about light affecting moods and emotions, but also about how it shapes the very world we observe. This is reflected in the "realisation that everything we see / is luminance" and also the emergence of colour into a grey world. The dashes of red suggested by the poppies and the lips referred to in the early part of the poem are transformed into the many colours of the beloved's eyes in the last stanza.

In writing poetry I have often gone through periods where I tried too hard and the poems either hid in the shadows or stood dully in the light. I realised with 'Photosynthesis', and in many subsequent poems, that I needed to trust my own voice more, to let the words make their own way out of the darkness, blinking in the sunlight.

RODY GORMAN

Imirce

Ag cuartú ar mo chuairt de ghnáth
Idir m'eol agus mo thír,
Na corra ag teacht nuair a thagann geimhreadh
I gCuailgne agus i nGleann Aighle,
An breac bán ag gluaiseacht suas an tSionainn san earrach,
Na feithidí aerga sa samhradh sa mhá,
An lon ag gluaiseacht anuas i ndeireadh an fhómhair,
An damh donn is an damh rua ag rith
Thar an ré thar bharr uachtair an fhéir
Nuair a thagann doineann agus fearthainn,
An cadhan is an giúrann os cionn Imleach Iúir,
Na sionnaigh bheaga sa sneachta,
Na mic tíre ag fágáil a n-adhbha
Chun dul ag seilg san oíche
Go Sliabh Fuaidh, an rón ramhar sa trá
Ag teacht ón muir in Inis Bó Finne,
Na héisc nuair a imíonn an t-oighear ar Loch Éirne
Agus mé féin ar fáinneáil is ar foluain.

Bodytransfermigration

Circuitsearching on my timevisitcircuit as usual eitherboth–
between my home range and familiar area, the oddroundherons
coming when winter comes in Cooley and Glenelly, the
fallowwhite poxtrout moving up the Shannon in spring, the
serpentbeastinsects of the air in summer on the mazeplain,
the ouzelelk coming down at the end of autumn, the Jovelord-
timberbrown and red championox-stag running across the
moonperiodplain over the creamcrophindrancetops of the
grass when winterstorms and the rains come, the barnaclegeese

above Emly, the little foxes in the snow, the landsonwolves leaving their den to go spleenhunting at night in the Fews, the fat horse-hairseal on the strand coming from the sea on Baffin Island, the fish when the ice has gone from Lough Erne and myself fannelfluttering and full-onfloatflying.

Translated by the author

This piece is from an ongoing sequence consisting of a version or *intertonguing* (the literal meaning of the Scottish Gaelic for translation, *eadar-theangachadh*) and enlargement of the medieval romance *Buile Shuibhne*. This version (or subversion), entitled *Sweeney: An Intertonguing*, shifts in personae, time, locations and languages, primarily triangulated between English, Irish and Scottish Gaelic including past and present dialects (Cape Clear, Erris, Omeath, Rathlin, Ring, Tyrone etc.), and, to a lesser extent, Cant, French, Icelandic, Latin, Manx, Orcadian, Ulster Scots and Yola, in various forms of prose, verse and song as a sort of play for voices. The stratagems employed include *lingua gadelica* combining elements from both forms of Gaelic, phonetic rendering, round-trip translations of the responses of Heaney, Joyce, Muldoon, Mahon, Sweeney et al, recontextualisation (of, for example, 'Encounter' by Czesław Miłosz), onomastic flourishes, vocables and sound effects, haiku with pictographs, inventory poems, academic paraphernalia and a polysemantic form of English translation which I have devised to represent the semantic range of original Gaelic texts and chosen to call Sweenese.

Sweenese is the designation I have given to the polysemantic translations from Irish and Scottish Gaelic and, occasionally a synthetic *lingua gadelica*. The methodology is simple enough — to give all the semantic elements and connotations associated with a single Gaelic word and to place them in the best order in accordance with Coleridge's dictum. The variant polysemantic forms of a single word relate also to the theme of shape-shifting throughout the narrative. It might be said also that this shape-shifting and language shift correspond to the different aesthetic or intellectual levels of the poems. The constant revision of the text may also be considered a form of shape-shifting. In the version I have devised of the sequence, Sweeney is presented as being bipolar, bisexual, bireligious and bilingual (at least).

MARK GRANIER

Grip Stick

The man emptying bins on the prom might be my age,
though healthier looking, tanned, bare-armed
in a hi-vis jacket and black ski-cap.
He plucks at stray bits of litter with that familiar
metal rod with its Dalek pincer — the same

as the one I bought for my mother in Fannin's
some years before she died — a gadget
so starkly ingenious surely it's a branch
of a family tree of similar inventions, of Bakelite,
whalebone, leather, wood ... going back, back

to that afternoon in her nursing home
a year and a half ago, when I hold her hand
and feel it loosen then go slack, and call
the nurse, who says quietly 'yes, she's going ...'
and I look out the window

to see the usual glorious rubbish, clouds
not stopping their tumble over Killiney Hill's
huddle of slates and satellite dishes, while I am
abruptly in a different country — the vast
landscape of her open palm —

tiny in the grip of what gave way.

Julian Barnes observed that, if we live long enough, life "divides into those who have endured grief, and those who haven't. These divisions are absolute; they are tropics we cross." I crossed my Tropic of Grief when my mother died in 2012, shortly before her 94th birthday. Having lived with and cared for her for over two decades, I should have been as prepared as anyone can be; I was even holding her hand when she died. But as the moment quickened into actuality I felt the shock of a physical division — an ice-wall had snapped the past from the present so the latter was now a brand-new territory. Going to bed later that night, the duvet seemed pitifully inadequate to the interstellar chill, as did the ceiling, the house.

Life is a kind of weather: physical, political, emotional. Poets learn to keep an eye out for any serendipitous object that can be utilised as a makeshift lightning rod. The poem 'Grip Stick' wasn't planned. I wasn't hunting for a metaphor for grief. Instead, it signalled to me, in the form of a practical, everyday device my arthritic mother had used to retrieve objects near her bed or chair. Other applications for this device hadn't occurred to me till I saw the man on the prom in the poem's opening line. I was suddenly struck by the gadget's elegant simplicity. I wrote a few lines and soon found that the central image was mimetic; like the litter worker, it picked up things — images and phrases — connecting metaphorically with that moment by my mother's bed.

Although all art is artifice, a good poem will usually seem, in some sense, organic, impart something of Keats's insistence that it should have come "as naturally as the leaves to a tree". I don't know if 'Grip Stick' manages this but its metaphorical shifts in time and space felt rhythmic and right. It gathered and flowed into itself: stick, lightning rod, time-machine, palm.

VONA GROARKE

from Or to Come

'— *for the living know that they will die,*
but the dead know nothing.'
— Ecclesiastes 9

There are always unvisited corners
where the only sound is the turn taken by dandelions
or a robin rustling in the aftergrass nearby. Where
a wooden cross tied at the joint bears no name or date
and where what is absolved goes deeper than the darkening
rain where a cursory coat of whitewash has washed off.

The dear bouquets will have sweated a film of rust
inside their plastic domes, and the bare bones
of a handful of wild flowers in a jamjar hold their own.
It could be the churchless graveyard with a stile
at one end and a row of recent yews put down
to mark the high wall off the estate.

Where graves of couples, and the odd stray child
who died young and will forever pine for crisper
company than theirs to upbraid her elders
with her unused life, go unremarked
under the weight of memorials that are stained
with lichen and damp and generations of disregard.

Or an acre that knows the steady traffic of Sundays'
early Masses and, on holy days, Devotions.
Where the grotto with the kneeling, ashen girl is lit
at night by a halo in the crown
of the blue-robed figure with a bemused face.
The priest switches them on after evening Mass

as he makes the cross from his mutton and bungalow
to his divine estate. On All Souls' Night,
he leads a vigil in which a handful of headscarves
and a single girl give him back the answers
to have them wrapped up in 'Amen'.
The glow of the bulbs keeps them all in thrall

and gives them a look of pitted rhapsody, though
they are only counting beads on a length of chain
and feeling the cold in the far ambitions of their feet.
Inside, the truer candles wither in their bronze clasps.
Tuppence each. One pound would fill the whole of heaven
at Our Lady's feet in the earthy Men's Division.

/...

Come Tuesday morning, the caretaker will have
his work cut out with the stray papers and butt ends
blown on from the car part that will press against
the gates and corner stones or be tossed up
by a stray whim of the wind. He will take
to his rounds and his boots will impress the gravel

so there will be a shuffle that follows his progress
and breaks only when he stops to pick the wrapper
of a Ritchies mint from the lee side of a marble corner pier.
He tends the verges on the other days, and knows
the lie of the land and why the grass darkens on one patch
and why nothing will grow in another.

Every now and then he will sit on a headstone
of a small girl's grave, from where the fields are squat
and laid ou in their clean straight rows
right down to the bottomless lake
where three Johns will have to drown
before the end of the world. (He knows of two,

100

though one was JJ who went in after a ewe
and left no family to say for sure
what the letters of his Christian name stood for.)
For the rest of the week, the graves in his patch
are visited by the curious or bereaved.
He knows them, as he knows his care, to see.

By the boy, perhaps, who comes off the bus
a stop too soon to tell whoever will listen
about how quiet the house is and how hard it is
to get up when she isn't there
to call him again and to dampen
down his hair and wave him off.

Or the woman who comes in early
in all weathers with a bag of crumbs that she casts
on her daughter's grave to bring on the birds
that will keep the small girl company and the soil
picked clear for another while when she can't
be there to mind her for herself.

/...

Coming as I do from a family of country lawyers, there
always seemed to be someone in a dark jacket heading
out to a funeral. It's what happens, I suppose, and you
might as well enjoy yourself, should the opportunity arise.
Country funerals can be jolly enough affairs in their way, since
unlike the other social hinges of the mart and Mass, they usually
involve a heap of potato salad and ham sandwiches, maybe even
apple tart. Some say the ideal midland day out is a funeral in
the morning, a point-to-point in the afternoon, but I was never
much called on for either, for which I'm glad enough.

But I do love graveyards, and this poem is set in the one where both my parents are buried, though I suspect it could also be any Irish graveyard with its mix of forlorn and ordinary; its way of declaring the fact of death alongside small gestures of honouring it, or defying it. As if anyone could. Graveyards are where we are at our most ritualistic, and also our least guarded. People reveal themselves there, are candid in all kinds of ways they wouldn't indulge once they pull the gate behind them.

It's the longest poem I've ever written — thirty six-line stanzas extending over seven pages of a Gallery book. I used to threaten audiences with it in readings if they didn't behave themselves but I've never read it out loud, and not just because of the length. Stanza fifteen's depiction of a mother scattering crumbs to attract birds who will eat the worms that would otherwise defile her small daughter's body strikes me as unreadable. But it's also as something I wrote one time (sixteen years ago) that broke through a tone of melancholy not uncommon in my work, to something closer to the searing detail an honest poem will not flinch from.

It's a strange village, this graveyard, with its many flyblown lives and deaths, its buried narratives.

But that's poets for you, I suppose: ask me for a touchstone poem, I come up with a headstone one.

KERRY HARDIE

Life Gone Away is Called Death

This couple that we met who live in Dresden
sent us a book of photos of their city,
all taken when the war was near its end.

Sometimes the dead are sitting in the rubble
still warmly dressed in coats and hats and boots,
their shoulders resting casually together,

companionable, despite the strangeness,
the hollowing eyes, the skim of wrinkled milk,
the frame of bone just working to the surface.

I don't know why we need to live in bodies,
or why, when we have left, they hang around,
still stubbornly at home in linear time.

Some years ago I had a residency at the Heinrich Böll cottage. The weather was relentless. I was sharing the residency with my husband Seán, and we'd agreed to show no pity on the rain-drenched foreigners who all too frequently stalked the gate in the hope of gaining admittance. One day, hearing the sound of voices, I emerged from Böll's study to find Seán entertaining two dripping Germans who had — or so he explained a bit sheepishly — come all the way from Dresden to see the cottage. My welcome was unenthusiastic, but by this time he'd discovered that both of them worked for the police department, so curiosity rapidly overcame my annoyance and soon we were showing them round. Heinz was a police psychologist, while Andrea was currently head of the Dresden Department of Homicide. They spoke of police work before and after the Wall came down. Later we wondered if they had been Stasi. Stasi or not, they were both well worth the breach of our privacy.

When we got back to Kilkenny, Seán, who had interviewed Böll years before when he'd won the Nobel Prize, took a signed copy of one of the novels off our shelves and posted it to Dresden without telling me. I can't remember which of us answered the first phone call from the police department in that city, but I do remember my irritation when the calls didn't stop and a seemingly endless barrage of gratitude came flooding down the line.

'He was their hero,' Seán said when I complained. 'He meant so much to them. I knew we wouldn't even notice it was gone.'

We didn't, and he knew that wasn't what I was complaining about. The calls kept coming. They were accompanied by invitations and books, in one of which was a truly chilling photograph of a group of fully dressed adults sitting on the ground in a street in Dresden just after the fire-bombing. They were all dead — had probably died of suffocation when the oxygen in the air was eaten by fire. Their clothes were untouched.

MAURICE HARMON

from **The Doll with Two Backs**

It was a silence no one heard
no one talked about
a stillness that lingered

an absence in which what had been
was no longer felt
a loss no one was reckoning

in the faces of those he met
in the voices, the memories
in the mementos in house and barn

nothing he could put his hand on
nothing anyone could show him

saying this belonged to those who used to be
this implement, this bit of cloth, this worn moccasin
this pony, this remnant of a headdress

the landscape held its secrets
under the great pines
behind the falls, along the swift rivers

in the lichen and the water weed
an impenetrable stillness

'The Doll with Two Backs' began as an attempt to say
something about a journey to Oregon but expanded
into a story of a friendship between a visiting Irish

academic and a Native American girl. It resonates with the cruel treatment of Native American tribes and the way Irish tribes were treated during the Tudor and Elizabethan wars. It is a story of ignorance, invasion, broken treaties and harassment. Here and there the poem is grounded on historical realities.

It is a product of European culture. He is drawn to the history of the North West and puzzled by the disappearance of the Native tribes. She is part water nymph, part tree spirit, in tune with the natural world in the way her ancestors had been.

Their friendship begins promisingly but the poem moves from and through images of loss to the point where she opts out of what he represents.

I avoided a chronological narrative, feeling that its theme of disruption could be conveyed through a mosaic of incidents, scenes and voices. At the heart of the poem is the theme of storytelling, which was so much part of her culture and of his, of the failure of the imagination to absorb the Native American world.

He is the artist at the heart of his own story, trying to put the pieces together.

JAMES HARPUR

The White Silhouette

for John F. Deane

'*There went a whisper round the decks one morning, 'We have a mysterious passenger on board.' ... Often I thought of that rumour after we reached Jerusalem ... When I saw the man all in white by the Golden Gate carrying in all weather his lighted lamp, I always thought, 'There is a mysterious pilgrim in Jerusalem.'*
— Stephen Graham, *With the Russian Pilgrims to Jerusalem* (1913)

I thought we could meet in a holy place
Like the church in the hamlet of Bishopstone
Empty on a Wiltshire summer's day
The trees full of rooks and hung in green
And the stream in the meadows a rush
Of darkling silver beneath the bridge
Where I saw my first kingfisher flash
its needle, leaving its turquoise stitch
In my memory; where I would sit
In the church and close my eyes
And wait in vain for something to ignite
And wonder whether this was my life
Wasting away in my mother's home.
Sometimes I'd bring Herbert's *Temple*
And read the quiet order of his poems
And picture him, as once he was glimpsed,
Hugging the floor in his church at Bemerton
Asking love to bid him welcome.
I sat with an upright praying disposition
Preoccupied in self-combing
Too callow and spiritually impatient
To notice if you had slipped in
As a tourist to inspect the choir or font

And buy a picture postcard and sign
The book with 'lovely atmosphere';
Or as a walker taking refuge from rain
Or a woman primping flowers by the altar.

Or somewhere like the island of Patmos
Out of season and tourist flow,
The sea leeching blue from the skies.
In the cave of St. John, pointillist gold
On tips of candles and highlights of icons,
You might have visited that day in September
When I was there, absorbing the coolness,
Imagining John on the Day of the Lord
Prostrate on the ground as if before a throne
And you not dressed in a 'robe and gold sash'
Nor with hair 'as white as wool or snow'
But as a pilgrim with camera and rucksack
Respectful, curious, guide-book in hand
Appreciating the grain of raw stone
Catching my eye and pausing for a second
As if I were a schoolfriend from years ago.
I never saw you, if you were there,
For I was too blinded by the new Jerusalem
Flashing out jasper, topaz, sapphire
Descending from heaven like a huge regal crown.

Or somewhere like Holycross in Tipperary,
The abbey at the meeting of road and river,
You might have stopped to break a journey
As I often do, and seen me there in the nave
Ambling down the sloping floor
Towards the relic-splinter of the Cross
Or sitting outside on the banks of the Suir
On a bench on a swathe of tended grass
Perhaps that day when, heading north,

I paused by the car park to watch
A bride, fragile, and frozen by the door
Her bridesmaids huddled in the cold of March
Waiting and waiting to make her entrance
Into the sudden shine of turning faces
Like a swan gliding in its snowdress
From an arch of the bridge in a state of grace.
I was too mesmerised by her destiny
To see you start your car, drive off,
And raise your hand as you passed me by
On the way to Cashel, Fermoy and the south.

But there was that time I was so certain
That I had finally found you;
Sick at home, I turned to meditation
And prayer to overcome self-pity
For weeks accumulating quietude
Till that morning when seconds were emptied out
My thoughts cleansed, my self destroyed
Within an uncanny infusing light
That seemed to deepen and unfold
More layers of radiance and lay me wide open
So you could cross my threshold
Or I could cross, at any moment.
But I closed the door of my heart, afraid.
Who knows, that I might have met you
Afraid I would pass to the other side
And never return to all that I knew;
I thought I could always re-open myself
And greet you properly, well prepared.
I never did. I feared that sudden shift
Into the zone of timelessness; too scared
I looked for you in public, for safety,
I kneeled in churches, gave the sign
Of peace in St. James's Piccadilly,

I recited prayers, took bread and wine
And I concentrated so hard, but failed
To believe they were your blood and body;
I heard staccato prayers, like nails
Banged in, as if to board up windows.

Sometimes I'd sense you as a glimmer
As in that dream I once had out of the blue
When you stood at night on a Greek island shore;
Your face was hidden, but it was you;
The stars pinned in place the layers of darkness
Then came the comets, perhaps a dozen,
Their tails fanned out like diminishing sparks;
Slowly they twisted and turned — your hands
Moving in concert, as if you were guiding them,
As if they were on strings, like Chinese kites.
The comets slowed and stopped, and changed
Into letters of Hebrew, emblazoning the night.
And I knew if I could grasp those words,
Your silent message across the stars,
I'd know my destiny on earth.
Instead I woke, as puzzled as Belshazzar.

I do not search for you any more
I don't know whom to seek, or where;
Too weary, disillusioned, I'm not sure
What I think or if I really care
That much; my last hope — that my resignation
Might be a sign of the Via Negativa,
A stage of my self-abnegation —
That hope prevents the thing it hopes for.

And yet
I still write to you, poem after poem,
Trying to shape the perfect pattern

Of words and the mystery of their rhythm,
An earthly music audible in heaven —
Each poem is a coloured flare
A distress signal, an outflowing
Of myself, a camouflaged prayer
Dispatched towards the Cloud of Unknowing
And all I have to do is stay
Where I am, ready to be rescued
Not move, speak or think but wait
For the brightening of the Cloud
For your white silhouette to break
Free from it and come nearer, nearer,
Till I see your essence and I can ask
Where in the world you were
Throughout my days — and only then
Will I grasp why I never found you
Because you were too close to home
Because I thought I'd have to die
To see you there, right there, removing
The lineaments of your disguise —
My careworn wrinkled skin
My jaded incarnation of your eyes —
My face becoming your face
My eyes your eyes
I   you   us   I you us
Jesus

The idea of something beyond the self, such as a god, or the
Muse, providing poetic inspiration is no longer assumed;
perhaps it wasn't even in Virgil's day. But the idea is no
stranger than the notion of prayer (irrespective of whether one
practises it or not): the attempted communication with the
divine and the patient expectation for something to arrive from
'the beyond'. As those who pray hope for deep, spiritual solace,

poets who take their cue from the Muse naturally hope to arrive at deep, spiritual truths, even if the latter arrive in a confused or fragmentary state.

The key, perhaps, lies in the waiting — for the unlooked-for, looked-for, thing to arrive, and that perhaps happens only with a heightened awareness. We can know a person for many years before a shift in sensibility causes us to fall in love with him or her. It's a state of being that's found in the form of Greek divination known as kleidonomancy. Questioners would whisper their requests into the ear of a statue of a god and then proceed to the market place. The first 'random' overheard conversation they heard supplied the answer to their question. It relied on being faithful and being alert, just as poets have to be. This is hard to sustain. Mostly we blunder around with Blake's 'vegetable eyes', unaware of the great mysteries, or mysterious people, that pass us by. The Bible expresses this well in the story of Jesus on the road to Emmaus. He falls in with two disciples who fail to recognise him until he later breaks bread with them at an inn: 'Then their eyes were opened and they recognised him.'

MICHAEL HARTNETT

That Actor Kiss

I kissed my father as he lay in bed
in the ward. Nurses walked on soles of sleep
and old men argued with themselves all day.
The seven decades locked inside his head
congealed into a timeless leaking heap,
the painter lost his sense of all but grey.
That actor kiss fell down a shaft too deep
to send back echoes that I would have prized —
'29 was '41 was '84,
all one in his kaleidoscopic eyes
(he willed to me his bitterness and thirst,
his cold ability to close a door).
Later, over a drink, I realised
that was our last kiss and, alas, our first.

died 3 October 1984

My head is full of Ó Rathaille, Haicéad and Ó Bruadair, 'buckeens', as they might say, that I've been 'wrastling' with for a long time. Though he was instinctively pagan, the only recorded signature we have of Ó Rathaille is on a manuscript he copied of the priest/poet Seathrún Ceitinn's *Foras Feasa Ó Éirinn* in Drumcollogher in 1722.

Priest and poet are joined at the hip, history made outcasts of them both, scrounging for patronage, for audience, for a place in society. The priest and the poet are tramps down through history, but held in high — and this is the point — mystical esteem by the people. Haicéad was a troublesome article, a priest and a poet — his *Musgail do Mhisneach, a Bhanbha* was an apologia for the 1641 rebellion.

They were men of their time, as we are of ours. They lived their art, poetry was a way of life with them, a calling that could drive a man demented. Look at Ó Bruadair — not a lifestyle choice, a 'sideline' like you have now.

If you were to push me for a favourite [poem of my own], I'd have to go with 'That Actor Kiss', in memory of my father who died on the third of October 1984.

(St. Ita's Day, Jan. 15th, 1999)

Nightmare

A cobalt night in blue relief
and the hunt begins.
The green grass black
and the talking baby frightens me.
Bug-eyed horrors hover in
our shadows, lingering, carnivorous.
Wailing now to let him stay.
He stumbles after, the talking baby.

Drop under the yickety-yackety picket fence.
A treacherous fork in the road.
I know well the dangers.
Where I go the baby follows.
I urge him back to the black-green grass,
behind the yickety-yackety picket fence.
'You'll be safer there', I promise.

He crawls back under with pleas
to follow. We neither saw the pit
that he fell in, in velvet silence. A
small hand held the edge but
slipped away beneath my grip.
A cobalt night in blue relief
and the hunt begins.

I hope my poetry encourages a reader to imagine otherness. From the instant my poem is alive in the imagination of the reader, I would like it to own its existence, to engage all the senses, and not merely be a deliberation on likeness. Successful poems, I believe, leave a residue in the afterthought of the reader.

Years ago, as an experiment, we took black and white photographs of February daffodils, tipped the flower heads with yellow ink, and watched how our mind's eye turned the grass green, the trees brown. Language in poetry can achieve a similar effect.

In 'Nightmare', the green grass becomes black, and has a talking baby stumble over it. A benign, safe image suddenly becomes sinister.

I like to create cinematic-like flow in poems, with twists and turns as the poem apparently reveals whilst in fact concealing. That is not to say the poem should trick the reader, although it is quite legitimate to puzzle.

It is only in the final stanza of 'Nightmare ...' that the possibility that the poem might be about loss is revealed. South African poet, Don MacLennan wrote, "a poem never drains / its ground of silence". 'Nightmare's' version of loss, not withstanding its terrifying world, is one with which many readers can identify.

My natural tendency is towards literalness, which I try to use to advantage in my writing. In my poem 'The Present', about times past and present, I go inside a clock to visit each themed room of my history. In 'Nightmare', I go deep into the cobalt night of the unconscious.

BREDA JOY

November Morning

i.m. Joe Owens

Between the conifers and the commonage
the dogs run ahead on sodden ground,
rain behind me, more to follow —
steel-wool skies and delinquent squalls.

Even the splendour of frost on Mangerton's shoulder
cannot gladden me. Nor can the sudden burst
of a red stag from the wood, swaying antlers
the tribal headdress of a warring chieftain.

I watch him in flight,
moonwalker light, clearing
the boundary ditch while a pheasant
explodes in bronze and carmine

from a mound of mouldering dung
and arrows towards the wood —
power of deer and bird straining
either end of an invisible line.

My eyes track the monarch, his rusted
bulk dissolving into a winter canvas
of alder, faded furze
and amber River Caol.

He harries me beyond mired thought,
delivers me to the parched page,
disappears into this aboriginal land
I have trespassed on.

C all it melancholy, call it apathy, whatever label you choose to fix on it, there was some malaise weighing down on me that rainy morning I walked my father's land in the Muckross area outside Killarney with my dogs, Patch and Sam.

The frosted beauty of Mangerton Mountain and the sudden burst of the stag, so solitary and splendid, failed to move me. I watched the stag speed towards the commonage while, at the same time, the pheasant flew in the opposite direction; the energy of both appeared to create a tension along an invisible line.

It was only when I was trying to track the passage of the stag through the commonage that I experienced a moment of insight that lifted me out of myself and became the genesis of this poem.

I was reviewing my/our relationship with the wild red deer of Killarney, a species first recorded in Ireland 26,000 years ago. The encounter with the stag challenged the 'notions' we have of ourselves as human beings — our sense of superiority to other creatures, of ownership of the planet we share.

The insight made even more sense when I later learned that we only arrived on this boggy footprint on the edge of Europe about 9,000 years ago.

If he could have spoken, the monarch of Muckross might have bellowed, "Get over yourself". Yet, his provocation of an original variation on the thoughts carouselling round my head did just that — wordlessly. I got over myself to such an extent that I drove home and sat down to write after yet another absence from the page.

The following day I got a phone call to tell me of the passing of Joe Owens, Scotsman, journalist and coal miner, who mattered so much to me.

BRENDAN KENNELLY

from **Antigone**

Man, genius, wit, prophet, poet,
Thinker, worker, sage,
Controls the hearts of birds in flight,
The hearts of prowling beasts,
Beasts roaming the hills.
He tames the wildest creature,
Makes him accustomed to the yoke.
Man is strong and wise and beautiful.

He tames the mountain bull.

He tames the wild life of words
The mad life of thought
All the dangerous moods
Of heart and mind.
He copes with frost and hail and rain.
He does not flinch from pain.
Only death defeats him,
Death, master of the master.

It's the simplicity of *Antigone*, a play that I published in translation in 1996, that interests me. Interests or, should I say, haunts me, as do its many translators, an eclectic bunch ranging from Freud, Brecht to Hegel — each generation has to engage with this play.

"True progress is possible only between opposites," according to Blake. Antigone and Creon, the personal and the public face of justice, in one respect, are both righteous, passionate people: what sets them at odds with each other is their attitude towards the dead.

Antigone suits the Irish temperament, the Kerry in me that looks back and is haunted by the village, the stark reality (not necessarily harsh) of the place I grew up ... a material world that judged harshly like Creon but had its tender side like Antigone.

Greek world-view is always direct, engages with the 'reality' of the human condition. The hole in the rock that Antigone is condemned to live out her life in is not so exaggerated when you think of the atrocities of the world today and was possibly a 'suspended sentence' in ancient times.

What the Irish and the Greeks have in common is tribe, the pull of the ancestor. That we are not forgotten by the dead is why we remember, why every tribe builds ritual around the humans who have gone.

PATRICK KEHOE

The Nearness of Blue

The nearness of blue
At each turn in the road
From Messonghi to Boukari.

Fixed glimpses of the bay
Between houses and buzzing trees;
Light on the shimmering wave plateau,
The salt desert of the sea.

We finger the pulse of hourless night,
We walk under the high islands of stars.

During my first visit to the Greek island of Corfu, about ten years ago, I was idly looking at a book rack outside a souvenir/bric-à-brac tourist shop. Among the usual colour guides to the island, I happened to see a dusty paperback copy of a book unknown to me, a work entitled *Prospero's Cell*, written by Lawrence Durrell. It caught my attention for I knew of no decent literature about Corfu. In fact I knew little about the place at all.

When I got back to Ireland, I checked out Durrell's 140-page work and thus stumbled on perhaps my favourite book. *Prospero's Cell* is subtitled 'A Guide to the landscape and manners of the island of Corcyra' — Corcyra is the Greek name for the island rendered phonetically.

Prospero's Cell is like no other book, it seems *sui generis*. I think of it as much poetry as prose. Other Durrell travel books, such as *Bitter Lemons of Cyprus* and *Reflections on a Marine Venus,* are not quite as strong.

Durrell's enduring masterpiece is a respectfully informed and beguiling portrait of this green island, which is covered in large part with olive trees. The curious thing for me personally is that although this affectionate account recalled — mostly in diary format — the island as it was before the terrors of the Second World War, its essential spirit pervaded forever after my own particular sense of Corfu, though experienced many decades afterwards.

Thus I would always try, after further visits, to write poems about Corfu which aspired to the same air of hypnotic, somnolent calm and contentment that Durrell once conjured in his inimitable prose. It sure beat the constant watching of amateur YouTube films from Corfu that only frustrated, being without the scent and the atmosphere that is difficult to express in words. But Durrell managed the almost impossible feat.

HELEN KIDD

Sunspill

when the west licked
under the cloud low
silver, gold leaf prising
the sky lid so that
the grumpy driver, the
one-eyed dog, the early
drunks, the Japanese
tourist, the old man
at the front of the queue
were each in a luminous
pocket and the pigeons
and pensioners, and the
cyclists
and Friday night out
and the suddenly
antiphonal windows
all signalling
something else
something else
something else
and just for a moment
everyone's shoulders
grew wings.

Choosing a poem is like saying you have a favourite child,
it can't be done. So the most honest selection becomes
one which expresses the heart of what I believe in.
Sure I have poems about mountains, seascapes, art, love, loss,
music, dreams, ecology, politics and protest, poems for people

and about language and gender. I have traditional forms and experimental ones; what to do with all this?

'Sunspill' seems to cover the core of everything I hold dear. It is a people poem, insofar as it says everyone has something numinous about them. The 'luminous pocket' of the evening light is as much inside each of us as it is bestowed upon us, and it is completely egalitarian. I believe the creative potential of every human being is what 'soul' means. Everyone has it and it gives you wings.

You could call the moment an 'epiphany', and these are everywhere if we are attuned to them; but I won't limit with a name that which lifts us beyond the everyday. I am wary of boxes and labels; they can be linguistic pitfalls. But language also has infinite variety, so 'something else' is a litany that won't restrict that sense of the sublime.

It is expressed in the antiphonal number three, and occupies a space close to the use of the liturgical word 'antiphonal'. That's as near to religious diction as I dare go; mainly because call and response, shared uplift, is what antiphon suggests; more community than individual.

I am a woman who writes, and consequently I am sensitised to how language can hem us in, and how poetry can break us out of the boxes that convention constructs. This is a free-form poem for a freeing moment, and I didn't want to get in the way either of the moment, or of giving that moment to the reader, by saying 'me' and 'I'.

We share these moments, so that we might be better people.

This is my way of saying that, if we pay attention to it, everything really is fundamentally good. It's a small hymn to the something that keeps us connected. So the poem is spun out of the contrast of the mundane with barely tangible images, coupled with palpable sound textures (with which I am always enamoured).

It is composed of short run-on lines, and is only one sentence without any punctuation to rein it in, so that it can stay as airy and possible as it can. There's just one specialised word, and only one capital letter, and although it's the High Street, and busy, there are worlds meeting, travellers and locals, dogs and bus drivers, and every single one of them is as important as the others.

That's the mother-lode that underpins my politics, my writing, and what I try to live up to. It's all there, and the more we give it away, the more it grows, like poetry too I suppose.

NOEL KING

Black and Tan

My grandmother knew the opening scrape
of her front gate was not a friend,
told us she remembered staying perfectly still,
his hard steps crunching through her.
She didn't remember his face,
how long he stood in her kitchen,
what lies or truths she uttered
while my infant aunt gurgled in her cot.
She did remember his words:
I have a little girl like this at home, myself.
For sixty three years she stepped over
the spot on her flagged floor
where the Black and Tan had stood.

One of the opening poems in my debut collection, *Prophesying the Past,* 'Black and Tan' is a true story my late paternal grandmother told me.

It must have been the mid-'70s and I must have been doing something in history in primary school which must have brought up the subject of the Black and Tans. I sat in rapt attention as Nan Nan, as we called her, told me that one of them came to her house one day. I asked something like, "Here in this very kitchen?" and she nodded slowly: "Yes, on those very flag stones that you are standing on now."

Nan Nan said her "heart was in her mouth" when he seemed to dribble over the baby's cot in the corner of the farmhouse kitchen. The baby in question was my aunt Mary, who only passed away in October 2016, aged 95. I didn't think of writing a poem about it then. I didn't write poetry then. I didn't expect to ever write poetry (or anything else). Nan Nan died in 1979.

I started writing poetry in 1994 in a workshop given by the late Eithne Strong. I wrote 'Black and Tan' about 1998 or 1999. The original title was 'The Two-Tone Invader'. I sent it out a few times ('sent out' being the working poet's term for submitting work to magazines and journals, and getting rejected).

Then I tried Fergus O'Donoghue, then editor of the prestigious Jesuit journal *Studies*, which recently celebrated its centenary year. Fergus had this 'secret reader'; all poets who submitted work got back these wonderful handwritten-in-caps notes about their poems, with suggestions for improvement and it was he/she who suggested I just call the poem 'Black and Tan'.

In this decade of centenaries, the poem is my glance back to troubled times.

THOMAS KINSELLA

Marcus Aurelius

I *On the Ego*

Gaspbegotten. In shockfuss.
     Out of nowhere.

Bent in blind sleep
     over a closed book.

Through the red neck
     cast out,

his first witness
     the gasp of loss,

to lie spent a while
     in the bloodstained shallows.

A little flesh. A little breath.
     And the mind governing.

II

Affairs were troubled in those days,
with over-confidence and ignorance everywhere.
A citizen, absent a while on an undertaking,
would find only increased coarseness on his return.

He himself, notable in his time and place,
and a major figure as later times would agree
(though for reasons that would have surprised
                              his fellow citizens)
was in a false position:

                    cast in a main role,
while fitted with the instincts of an observer;
contending throughout his life with violent forces
that were to him mainly irrelevant.

Threatened on the Northern border by brutal tribes
with no settled homes — swift in the attack,
inspiring great fear; but ignorant and unskilled,
swift equally in the retreat —

these he dealt with, stemming their advance
and scattering them among their own confusions.
It was after his death that they resumed their incursions
that led to the break-up of the Western Empire.

A vaguer-seeming contagion out of the East,
more deadly in the longer term — in the citizens'
depths of will, and their dealings among themselves —
this he neglected.

                 Though it seems in retrospect
that nothing of any substance could have been done.
That it was irresistible
and in the movement and nature of things.

Called upon for decisive positive action,
at which he was more than averagely effective;
but preferring to spend his time in abstract inquiry,
for which he was essentially ungifted;

he kept a private journal, in Greek, for which
he is best remembered. Almost certainly
because it engaged so much of the baffled humane
in him, in his Imperial predicament:

accepting established notions of a cosmos
created and governed by a divine intelligence —
while not believing in an afterlife;

proposing exacting moral goals, with man
an element in that divine intelligence
— while pausing frequently to contemplate

the transient brutishness of earthly life,
our best experience of which concludes
with death, unaccountable and blank.

As to the early Christians, who might have helped
with their new simplicities, he took no interest,
unsystematic in their persecution,
permitting the martyrdoms to run their course.

III

Faustina, wife of Marcus, developed a passion
for a certain gladiator. She confessed this
to her husband, who had the gladiator killed
and his wife bathed in the blood. They lay together,
and she conceived and brought into the world
the son Commodus, who grew to rule
with Marcus for a while as Emperor,
and became sole ruler on Marcus' death
— coming to terms quickly with the Northern tribes.

His rule was arbitrary, bloody-minded,
centred on the Games; and culminated
in the belief that he was Hercules.
His plan to appear for an Imperial function
in the arena, dressed as a gladiator,
led to public outcry, and his assassination,
strangled in private among his close advisers.
His death, succeeded by chaos and civil war,
ended one of the Empire's longest periods
of civic affluence and stability.

We are living in curious times, it seems to me, times of extraordinary change, both global and affecting the individual. We heard this afternoon* poems from Pádraig J. Daly, poems of great emotion about the fading of belief. The actual foundations are shifting.

Looking some time ago for a way of expressing these upheavals I found myself in Ancient Rome; with the figure of Marcus Aurelius. A curious case, for curious times. An emperor in the wrong job. Most comfortable at the edge of things, keeping a memorable diary, he was caught up in demanding, continental violence. Worrying with his own problems of belief, a great historic, emblematic figure towards the close down of the Roman Empire.

The poem is in three parts; the first a short birth poem, finishing with words from Marcus Aurelius himself. The second is political, and says something about contemporary Ireland and the world as I see it. The third I will leave to your own judgment.

(* *Transcribed introduction to a reading of the poem in Belmullet,* *Co. Mayo, June 2006*)

JESSIE LENDENNIE

Quay Street, Galway

There are ghosts on Quay Street.
Not the Claddagh ghosts,
who looked for company
late crossings on the bridge
to the old place,
but my ghosts
left behind on Fairhill,
wondering where I am
why the light flickered
why I can't find my way home.

This poem incorporates some ideas that obsess me: loss, displacement, change and identity. When I was very young I was fascinated with how the horizon merged into the cotton fields around our house in rural Arkansas. I had a strong sense of being there and elsewhere at the same time. This comes to me at times as a sense of loss; an unending journey in search of self and what I can call home.

JOHN LIDDY

Scarecrow

I have heard the egg crack
In a wren's nest. The wind snap
At the thistle tip of every sting.
Once there were two spiders

On a quilt of toasted leaves,
Each with its own blueprint
For its own invisible web.
One hunter I knew would kill

A fox before his gun sniffed
The scent. I have seen a river
Doll tug free from those stones
Born on river beds and challenge

The battering course of another
Journey. I have cheered the walk
And tumble of a foal in her
Mother's blood, cursed those boots

That crushed the ripe stalks
Of my pride. I am a scarecrow
Nailed to old wood, eaten
By worms, paralysed by rust.

I grew up with scarecrows. The neighbouring farmers employed them to protect their crops and there was one in particular whose path I frequently crossed on my walks through the fields with a neighbour's dog, Toby, or our Springer Spaniel, Nessa.

Entire days were spent exploring the Rookery, the Fairy Fort and the secret grove where Mr. Clancy cut his walking sticks from the hawthorn bushes to sell to the American tourists. After each foray I would sit on the bank of Carney's stream and let the dogs wash off the muck of the day's adventure, while I jotted down some ideas for poems.

One late summer's evening, crossing the field where the scarecrow stood guard, I saw Nessa growling at the solitary figure, circling and taunting, baring teeth, the hairs standing on her neck. It was the first time she had paid any attention to the scarecrow. I wondered what had spooked her.

On other walks, I was puzzled why Nessa never went near him again. Perhaps he had been annoyed with the dog's intrusion and was just doing his job? So, I entered the scarecrow's world to find out, and the poem contains what I discovered.

Some people have read the poem as a comment on Ireland, which I don't deny. I prefer, however, to remember it as my first, carefully constructed nature poem, achieving the possibility of 'seeing things' as Seamus Heaney would later put it, and playing with internal rhyme, use of onomatopoeia and enjambment.

In that sense, it was a breakthrough poem that allowed for an imagined response to my surroundings, written around the mid 1970s, enabling me to later weave my own multi-coloured quilt, with many a nod since to the natural world.

ALICE LYONS

Arab Map of the World With the South at the Top

Ibn Hawqal, 10th century

Plainsong puzzle.
No rush to mean.
Duodenum inlet.
Dotty. Green.

Holes in the hills.
Oval worldview.
Hawqal on a roll.
Foiled fold snafu.

Truro on the ulna.
Truro on the ulna.

Terre vert, vinegar,
Urine, honey, salt.
Lambent vellum riff.
Simmered down gestalt.

Trouble on the sea.
Bug proboscis cay.
Bang a left east
To slack-jaw bay.

Truro on the ulna.
Truro on the ulna.

I had an extended Early Map Phase. Postcards, books, glass cloths, even mousepads which depicted any visual attempt to represent a world pre-Quattrocento filled my home and studio. The phase roughly coincided with my relocation from an East Coast U.S. metropolis to a rural North Roscommon village. The early maps chimed with my need for estrangement, for poking holes in my habitual ways of living, for putting the South at the Top. It was also a time when I drew and wrote in equal measure, moving fluidly from one mode to another.

I loved how Ibn Hawqal, in chalky, olive-coloured paint, fumbled on vellum toward representing the known and unknown places, quite the way a child might. I copied all my favourite early maps over and over in my notebooks, in my paintings. I tried to write poems that groped in language the way that Hawqal and his crew groped with their brushes and their pigments made of tinted earth, honey, vinegar, urine and salt. Toward making "a world, a breather" (Christopher Middleton).

What a relief, these images that don't know any better, that are chancing their arms, geographically.

And speaking of arms, the refrain of my poem, "Truro on the ulna, Truro on the ulna", refers to the way New Englanders talk about Cape Cod. They make a muscle-man arm (Woods Hole is near the armpit, Provincetown the fist) and they point to their destination. Truro is along the ulna.

The body can be a map.

'Truro' and 'ulna' are weird words.

I tended toward the cerebral but I wanted to wriggle out of book knowledge because I didn't fully trust it. I trusted fumbling, feeling, groping, playing—not so much to recover radical innocence as to create conditions for radical stumbling. For exploration.

AIFRIC MacAODHA

Gabháil *Syrinx*

Critheann an solas
Ar chothrom an locha,
Ritheann an ghealach
Den chiorcal róchumtha.

Stopann fad spéire
Fán aimhréidhe theann,
Ropann a loinnir
Inneach na gcrann.

Feileann an t-iomlán
Do theorainn na luachra.
Ceileann an chiumhsóg
Tosach an bhruacha.

Ligim uaim le haimsir
Pictiúr seo na bruinnille:
Ní ghéilleann sí d'éinfhear
Ná ní sheasann ina choinne.

Anáil mhná, ní scaoileann
Ach eadarghlór ar tinneall:
I láthair na gabhála,
Ceiliúrann sí is critheann.

The Taking of Syrinx

Light flickers
on the lake surface
and the moon flies
the glamoury circle.

A length of unmoored
sky defies strong
snares and the trees'
weave is torn by lustre.

The whole sets off
the rushy edge,
the narrow bounds where
the river-bank ends.

Over time I develop
this picture of the girl:
she yields to no man
nor stands in his way.

A woman won't breathe
unless ready, between-words:
at the site of the ambush,
she sways, transformed.

Translated by David Wheatley

There is, or used to be, a painting of the Greek myth of Syrinx, hanging in the hall at Lissadell. I remember the tour guide running through the story and recognising as a teenager, in a separate, intimate way that I would write something on Syrinx, that I would definitely make use of her three jumps from nymph to reed to reed pipe.

Because the past six years have been full of false starts and dead ends, it has been interesting for me to look back and see how many drafts the poem 'Gabháil Syrinx' stipulated — three red A5 Staedtler notebooks, in fact. It's good to know that I'm wrong, that things never came easily, not even then.

It will be a while before I dip into the myth-kitty again, I hope, but if I'm even-handed, I suppose two things might rescue my early poem. Around the time I visited Lissadell, I came across the expression 'anáil mhná' (woman's breath) in a Medieval Irish tale. In it, a wife reproaches her husband for not realising that their daughter is returning, for the first time, from a lover's bed: "Wake up," she says, "yours is a bad sleep. Listen, our daughter now breathes a 'woman's breath'." The phrase was a chance discovery and I'm glad it's in there, in with the reed pipes and the will-I, won't I's of my nymph's progress.

The word 'ceiliúrann' in the last verse might just save me too. The verb 'ceiliúir' means to 'celebrate' — but it also means to 'vanish' or to 'disappear'. Given that poetry now appears to roundly and visibly celebrate itself, I'd have to admit that I don't entirely regret that tentative, self-conscious verb.

JENNIFER MATTHEWS

Work Out

TV1: SIERRA LEONE ON LOCKDOWN.
TV2: A man clutches a woman's ponytail, a horse's rein.
I set the elliptical to intervals.

EBOLA VIRUS COULD BECOME BIOTERRORIST THREAT.
She'll eat your heart out ... like Jeffrey Dahmer.
I make a comparative study of other women's arms.

50 SHADES OF GREY HIT THE 400 MILLION MARK.
A woman plays cello in a black lace bra.
Over the waistband my belly sags, an awning in a rainstorm.

TWITTER FEUD DESTROYS MY LIFE.
Yes I'll be whatever you tell me when you're ready.
I increase my resistance to 8, start to lose my breath.

I'm an insomniac. All vision, poetic and otherwise, is filtered through this state. Living between wrecked wakefulness and restless dreaming is something most poets have in common. Mostly it is 'Ugly' that keeps me up at night: ugly words, physical atrophy, polite campaigns of isolation, grotesque politicking, behind the scenes bullying and the silence that enables personal violence.

Writing is my forensic investigation of what disturbs me when I must be awake. Whenever possible, I try to look at my own complicity. Unravelling bandages, I ask the injury what where when how who why? If the injury talks back, if I shut up and listen, the poem will be good.

A formative concept for me came when studying the poetry of Anne Bradstreet in school. My teacher told us about the diaries that Puritans kept which were part confessional, part conversation — a wrestling with — God. Writing was a devotional, daily practice. Not in a comfy, have-a-cup-of-tea-with-Jesus way; it was taking an honest look at one's failings in the hope of being spared hellfire.

Poetry is my devotional wrestling with Human Creators, and this world we've crafted in the image of our own psyches. I would like to leave my investigation of Ugly, and sit down with Beauty. I want to meet Keats's "still unravish'd bride of quietness", or find myself 'Rowing in Eden' on a Dickensian wild night. I have this feeling that, if I could just sleep, poetry might look a little different. I will know I have grown as a poet when I can add to my devotional a practice of observing Beauty, becoming a Human Creator that crafts images of a life worth waking for.

JOHN McAULIFFE

Today's Imperative

after Horace, Ode 1:7

Others have herblife, bogland, the bird sanctuary.
Or manmade canals and urban decay.

And they have international flights of fantasy too:
But wherever they go,

It all looks and sounds the same to me,
Mountains, some work, a nice sunrise that none of the other
    tourists sees

Or an epiphany that signals a deeper
Engagement with the local patois/native literature.

Then there are the argonauts
Who labour in the interstices of a language, or two at most;

And that crowd whose ambition is to introduce gender
To the reader who hasn't got one on her:

Long warm-ups, agreed movements from *a* to *b*, and put up
    the shutters
With a lyrical turn or various little-known fabrics and figures,

Such as you often find in those who use family detail as glitter
To stud the rough black rock of their fictions.

And I like all this, but
It doesn't live in me, it doesn't wake me up in my skin at night

I'd rather sing to you about what's imperative,
So, listen. Take your mind off the stresses and anxiety of life

And whether you're in a southern town
Like Cork or Montpelier, or even Washington or Rome —

Go pour yourself a glass of wine.
Now. Imagine the kind of man who trusts himself to fortune

And says: 'Let us go wherever it takes us.
We've heard that a better life awaits us *and* we've seen worse.

Today, banish worry, exile it, the night's young now
And soon we'll be back to the grind, in fact, maybe tomorrow ...

Cork and Montpelier

Today, banish worry, exile it, the night's young now
And soon we'll be back to the grind, in fact, maybe
tomorrow ...

I was living in Cork in 2000 when Justin Quinn and David
Wheatley started publishing some of my poems in *Metre*,
which was my idea then (and now) of an ideal poetry
magazine.

Quinn and Wheatley commissioned well-argued essays and
pointed reviews and they also published an array of sharp, smart
poems from both well known and new writers. I could never
really predict which writers it would be enthusiastic about and
I looked forward to its arrival in the post in the same way that
I looked forward to getting a new book by a favourite writer. As
well as giving me new 'favourite writers' it helped me to articulate
much more clearly the kind of poem I did not want to write.

143

It's very hard to keep a magazine at that level without its tapering off into special issues and 'schools' of writing but *Metre* managed to do so for about 7 years. This poem came out in issue 12, towards the end of its run, when I had already published a few poems there, and I was sure as soon as I started writing 'Today's Imperative' that I wanted it to appear in *Metre*. Although the poem is obviously based on Horace's poem, I think it was also inspired, almost as much, by the magazine's confidence that it could survey the world of poetry and, to some extent, take its measure.

In Horace's poem, which praises his home landscape in relation to other places, I found a poetic model for the critical overview that I so enjoyed when I read a good magazine. I especially liked the way at the end of the poem that Horace somehow manages to turn away from one set of landscapes without just condemning them, a very useful trick, choosing to say 'both/and' instead of 'either/or', which is what the poem does when it says "And I like all this, / but it doesn't live in me …" And the place names, Cork and Montpelier, New York and Rome, were meant to register that same nice confounding opening up of the world.

I'm still interested in writing poems that re-use existing models but I want to jam those models into a different shape, or imagine something different that can develop or take that existing material somewhere new. Maybe it's because I've always worked as a teacher, but I'm very conscious that most poems are copies — or at least start off as copies — of other people's poems, or of 'things as they are' in the world, but I'd like to think that poems should also be places where something new can still be made to happen.

It seemed to me then that a 'version' is a perfect vehicle for that idea, especially a so-called 'free' or opportunistic translation like this. There's another poem in the first book which is a translation of a Douglas Hyde poem, which was itself an English translation of an Irish-language poem, which was itself a version of an old story and, in that one, I liked very much the idea that translating from one English (Hyde's) into another English (mine) would isolate not what was 'true' or faithful in writing but what was original or imagined.

JOAN McBREEN

My Father

My father
was a lonely man
whose fifty years
at sea
had left
no deeper blue
in his eyes.

Once in spring
at Lissadell
he picked bluebells
for my mother
and his eyes
looked different.

He fought
death
a frightened man,
hauled
to unknown rocks
from an ocean
he could
not navigate.

I wonder nights now
what lonely bay
he sails in
and does he
quote his lines of Yeats
and smoke his pipe
and drink the whiskey
for the pain.

After my father, Bernard Collery, died in November 1986, I wrote the poem, 'My Father' as an elegy and in memory of his life as a ship's engineer who worked particularly during the war years for Irish Shipping. In the poem I tried to capture his love of Sligo and in the end his fight against the Grim Reaper. Sadly this poem, nor indeed any of my poetry, did not appear in print before his death.

Both my parents were great lovers of Yeats and of the flora and fauna of Co. Sligo. Readers of my work will find this legacy reflected in many, many of my own poems. Over and over I turn to the natural world as a starting point, and very often I have then moved on to themes of loss and grief.

The place name, Lissadell, was a very important one for me to use in the poem. Of course, the greatest influence on my poem came from the famous W.B. Yeats poem, 'In Memory of Eva Gore-Booth and Con Markievicz'.

Also having been a child and young girl living in Sligo, I have powerful memories of the bluebell woods at Lissadell and the sight of the strand there bounded on one side by Ben Bulben and across the bay by Knocknarea. It was, in the days of my youth, a place where the townspeople of Sligo went in all seasons to walk, to dream and to remember the historic house and the Gore-Booth family.

Thankfully, all this can once again be enjoyed by thousands of people from all over the world, thanks to the vision of Edward Walshe and his wife, Constance Cassidy, who have restored and opened the house and gardens to the public.

THOMAS McCARTHY

The Garden of Sempervirens

We've been in this small room since daybreak.
I look out on America, sunlight on the great plain
Of a neighbour's roof, on Ojibwa spirit
Racing by. We lie at ease for our own sake.
The frenzy of late March or a nineties puritan
Need for work can't move us from our perch.
You do move your arm, a little numb
From the weight of me. We both talk of home

And how we must go back. But for now
We are as numb as a young prisoner in Portlaoise
Who hears these words for the first time, amnesty, ceasefire.
At five thousand miles we manage somehow
To find a new vocabulary for peace.
Peace, like light, is almost too much to bear.
After so many years, how to come into the sun,
Pull the harrow from the brambles, set to garden.

From this bed where we made love I can see
More than a few winter creatures basking in light.
A college mower goes by, but squirrels hang on.
Late March America is theirs completely;
All ten thousand lakes and a thousand islands
Our own life has the sandalwood vapour of night
Marked with the fresh touch of your mouth,
Love and story, the accent of the South.

Yet what I might have written was suspended
The way yard work is in a Minnesota winter.
We held our breath. Now, see the winter heads of Clematis
The winter colour of Bergenia, or Skimmia,

With its white panicles of fragrance up ended.
We see again the private lust of poems and paralysis
Of poetry in a time of war, and how, undeterred.
Buxus keeps its shape, year after year, in memoriam.

There are a number of poems that survive like children, favourite creatures, over the years, so it is very difficult to pull one from that small group. The poem sequence 'The Sorrow Garden', written after the death of my father remains a strong presence for me, as does 'The Phenomenology of Stones', a Gaston Bachelard saturated love poem for Catherine.

But there are others, 'Mr Nabokov's Memory', 'The Dying Synagogue at South Terrace', 'Shroud' and 'The Waiting Deputies'. But if I had a choice between 'The Phenomenology of Stones' and 'The Garden of Sempervirens', the latter is the one, I think.

It is a poem from *The Lost Province* published in 1996. It was written while we were still in America, at Macalester College in Minnesota. It is about that unusually early spring of 1995, a real spring in Minnesota, and a metaphorical spring in Ireland.

But for now

'We are as numb as a young prisoner in Portlaoise
Who hears these words for the first time, amnesty, ceasefire.
Our own life has the sandalwood vapour of night
Marked with the fresh touch of your mouth.'

These were the heady days of the IRA ceasefire, days of extraordinary hope not only in Ireland but in Irish America. It is now difficult to recapture the sheer joy of Irish America in those days the pride in an Irish peace, the overwhelming enthusiasm for everything Irish in the American media.

History turned and the historic moment became a personal moment. Or vice versa. A little over a year before I'd interviewed

149

Gerry Adams for a feature in the Cork published *Stet* journal. Adams had just published his short story collection *The Street.*

There was a feeling at that moment that even the most minor person could participate in the developing historic moment. The poem is charged with that feeling of hope, of love, of an enduring domesticity. And the image at the end, the common box hedge buxus sempivirens is inserted into the poems as a sign of endurance.

It is one of the few poems of mine that I return to frequently. It describes a special time, the end of a long winter, the beginnings of hope.

PHILIP McDONAGH

Water is Best

Shining candles will be
Lit in each window
And a fire of turf
On each hearthstone kindled.

—Máirtín Ó Direáin,
'Cuireadh do Mhuire' ('Invitation to the Virgin')

THIS LANDSCAPE JOGGED by the Atlantic,
her island-hood
nuanced by causeways,

wasp's bellies of stone, requires
no definition,
existed always.

That sudden flash on the Italian
website, the news
of some *ennesima*

strage, some umpteenth massacre,
a bomb has caused
in the Baghdad bazaar,

will not re-orient our day
persisting rainy
in Indreabhán. Our lens

to construe hope is un-performing
light on *carraig*
and *cloch* that no bomb rends.

SOME SAY THE PLENTEOUSNESS of time
in Connemara,
or when the hunger lays

tenuous fingers on bare slopes
around Darjeeling
or loiters in some haze

of Africa, is consequent
on a complete
conquest; as if the soul

fumbled both knives and reasoning.
But here, within
decorum, is the avowal

of what might be and of an old
story ignoring
noise and aggrandisement:

grey are the waters of the mind
when rulers read
reticence as assent.

THE CHEMICALS THAT FIX the colours
in blocks of cloth
produce a harsh excess

that in the aftermath requires
our counterpoise.
Nature is in distress,

we give support by engineering
Nature's own gifts
to make things right. We fix

a compost made of worms and ordure,
herbs and live plants,
above a filter, a mix

of stones, grit, sand. The noxious liquid,
faced by our feat
of reason, runs its course:

through the set strife of organisms
it flows purged,
cleansed by a natural force.

BUT WATER'S PUREST image must
rise up, a form
before the shaping eye,

if love with natural elements
is to combine
and dyes and dyes' dregs die.

The glittering mirror of salt sea
was dark, Odysseus
walked on with heavy oar:

others' indifference to that curve
and potency,
the sign he waited for.

*Beidh coinnle geala i ngach fuinneog
lasta* — Ó Direáin
has pictured for us how

candles could burn in every window
and wanderers
find welcome, even now.

'Water is Best' has four sections. From each section to the next, the argument of the poem makes a leap. In the first section, I want to suggest that contact with nature, with an unsullied creation, is a source of hope:

Our lens

To construe hope is un-performing
light on carraig
and cloch that no bomb rends

In the second section, I examine the point of view of the coloniser. The coloniser is a child of the scientific revolution and is highly organized. To him, peoples living closer to nature have a dreamy detachment and an indifference to the dominant historical narrative; this fits them to be ruled by others. But I challenge this. A feature of the innate sense of justice is that it does not require us to say everything straight out or to act in the particular piece of theatre the ruler has in mind:

grey are the waters of the mind
when rulers read
reticence as assent

Section Three of the poem is based on an ecologically safe process for disposing of toxic waste that I saw in operation in a small textile business near Jaipur.

In the 21st century, for the first time in human history, we cannot take 'nature' for granted. What we call 'nature' needs buttressing by means of restraint and conservation. We make many interventions:

Nature is in distress,

we give support by engineering
Nature's own gifts
to make things right

Section Four addresses the fundamental question for a society with the capacity to engineer even human life itself. Is it possible to distinguish 'nature' from what is 'un-natural', the 'human' from the 'less than human'?

Is it possible to hold onto the belief that our lives can be brought into harmony with something antecedent to the work of our hands — something that we call nature?

The nub of the poem is provided by a story in Greek mythology concerning the last journey of Odysseus. Odysseus went on foot, carrying an oar. His journey would end when he found a people for whom his oar meant nothing:

> other's indifference to that curve
> and potency,
> the sign he waited for

I take this to mean that Odysseus, as his life drew to a close, no longer relied on skill or status or fame; instead he humbly submitted to a different kind of adventure, seeking contact with what I called earlier in the poem 'the plenteousness of time in Connemara.'

'Water is Best' is a phrase from Pindar's poem in which he compares the glory of a triumphant athlete to the purity of water.

Each of the four sections of the poem has six verses. In principle the stress pattern across the three lines of a verse is 4-2-3, giving nine iambic feet altogether. In each pair of verses the last words rhyme. On this tight structure I try to impose the rhythms of ordinary conversation.

Do not lie to a lover

but on the other hand,
do not always tell

the whole truth.
Sometimes your secrets will

feel like a fire beneath
your tongue, silently burning,

but they should be revealed
only when required,

like a cat's eye necklace
on a road's dark skin.

Disclosure exposes,
creates a stalking fear,

like that of the grasshopper,
who sang all summer

and now faces winter
without provisions,

as the wind whoops
and fleers,

and sleet skitters over
the whitening ground.

Although I wrote 'Do not lie to a lover' years ago, it was a breakthrough poem. My early default impulse was to write confessional poetry, but with this poem I began to understand how Emily Dickinson's advice to 'tell it slant' allows for mystery.

As I've had a varied upbringing in terms of exposure to landscapes, climates, cultures and languages, my imagery invariably cross-pollinates to include both urban and rural, African and Irish/European, and seasonal variations. I (often subconsciously) include body words. In this poem, even though only 'tongue' refers directly to the physical body, the words 'eye' and 'skin' are also used. (If you're counting, you could even include 'hand'!)

I like to pay attention to sounds. Here wind whoops and fleers, sleet skitters, the grasshopper sings and there is also the silence of restraint. In terms of the sounds of words, I am attracted to interspersed full rhymes, assonance and half-rhymes, such as grasshopper/summer; tongue/burning; fleers/skitters; winter/provisions; disclosure/exposes; mind/required; silent/fire etc.

My intention is for the dissonance between 'l' and 's' sounds, and the long and short 'i' vowel sounds to contribute to the idea of feeling an urge and holding it back. My poems frequently suggest something of a conflict.

I tend to write in tercets, or in single blocks, and I also prefer my lines to meander, to show "a mind thinking", as Elizabeth Bishop puts it. Earlier versions of this poem have appeared in both those forms. But I also like to experiment, and edit my work compulsively.

IGGY McGOVERN

Knight Errant

for my father

The cycle-clip you think you have mislaid
lies hidden in the old white crocker' jar
I cradle under blanket and brocade:
its jingle-jangle is my scapular.
Outside the last train shrieks a curfew call,
milk-bottle sentries settle for the night,
the evil dragon climbs the bedroom wall
and courage flickers like the landing light.
Before you come to exorcise my fear,
to count your blessings, wind your watch and say
that final bedside prayer on your knees,
you'll leave your work and gallop your *Destrier*
down Railway Road, free-wheeling all the way,
one trouser-leg a banner in the breeze.

There are five reasons why this poem marks a significant turning in my journey as a writer. First, it is a fully-rhymed sonnet, albeit somewhere between the stricter Petrarchan and Shakespearean forms.

I had worked my way religiously (and numerically) from the haiku through to the sestina before settling on this 14-line staple that still dominates my poetry — my most recent collection, *A Mystic Dream of 4*, is a sequence of 64 sonnets that tell the life of the 19th century Irish mathematician William Rowan Hamilton!

Secondly, it occasioned a major confidence boost in the rollercoaster of publication: I had been submitting to all the usual outlets and had one poem accepted by *Poetry Ireland*

Review for a themed issue on 'Sex' (one of the few issues to go to at least a second printing!). There was a launch at which I read my poem about my son's first pimple (a stretch, I suppose) and the readers were asked to read another poem if they happened to have one about their person.

I had just finished 'Knight Errant' and was delighted beyond words when the Editor asked if he could have it as well — a sweet moment! Thirdly, I am fairly sure that this was the first of my poems to feature the tricky first person pronoun — I still use 'him' sparingly but that bend needed to be taken.

Fourthly, the circumnavigation around my father continues to inform much of my writing — my latest attempt (a sonnet, of course) recalls how he singed my childhood eyebrows trying to rouse the fire with petrol!

Finally, it was my first encounter with the mysterium of poetry: I was one word short, a word for a bicycle that rhymed with fear? I opened the *Oxford English* randomly at 'D' to discover 'destrier' — a warhorse. Perfect!

MEDBH McGUCKIAN

Aunts

My aunts jived their way
through the '50s to my teens.
They lay till noon and called me up
to listen for their lovers at the gate,
and paid me for the colour of their eyes —
'Grey,' I said, or 'Brown,' when they wanted
blue or hazel, in their giggling,
sleeping-together dreams.

I watched them shading in their lips
from sugar pink to coral, from mulberry to rose,
and their wet skirts hungry for
the brilliance of their swing,
as they dried by the strange
elastic girdles, paper petticoats.

Once out of the blue
I caught them dancing on the bed,
with their undergrowth of hazel,
and their make-up sweated through.

I wanted to write for him one poem as cold and passionate as the dawn, or at least something along the lines of 'Mid-term Break' which is arguably everybody's favourite Heaney poem. The one that stands out grimly yet soothingly in a first collection whose 50th anniversary they celebrated solemnly last night. So it would have to be a brief play or drama, a short story or potted novel, with characters, scenes, narrative truth, speeches, activity, the shock of a deep emotional shock or what they call a steep learning curve, different moments laid one on top of the other in a social mosaic or family tragedy.

The speaker revisits an isolated isolating experience in which he is involved more as an observer listening and watching. My poem like his has a rural setting and charts a process of discovery, not of the accidental death of a younger sibling which forecasts the terrible killings to come, but of femininity, sexuality, dreams, music, colours, clothes. The car that Heaney gets a lift home in and the bumper that delivers the poppy bruise, is here the vehicle of romance that the ignorant or innocent child peers into for a high bribe — I was nine, maybe ten. The baby's cot or coffin is re-imagined as the twin beds on which the sisters revel in their eroticism: and yet there is a darker, buried substory behind the excitement, health and exuberance.

This bedroom, like Heaney's cottage, no longer there — it was deliberately burned down — without door, open to a rickety staircase, was the very one in which two elder sisters or aunts had themselves perished in the March of the big snow, 1947. I had heard my father say, from time to time, when it grieved him, that the walls were completely covered in blood. So the colours deepen, darken towards the menstrual mystery hidden at the heart of the skirts and underwear, sensed and intuited through the strong female smell offered as a mocking reward for voyeurism.

'Out of the Blue' was the name of a pamphlet shared by Paul Muldoon and Jimmy Simmons roundabout then. I did not understand the facts of Haworth Parsonage from my mother but from my father, my sister, and in this poem, four of my seven aunts.

JOHN MEE

Travel Light

pack everything you need
then throw away half
let's see what you've got
    luminescent, incandescent, evanescent
how long are you going for?
and all this
    sparkling, flickering, shimmering
what were you thinking of?
at the bottom
some heavier bits and bobs
    longing, falling, yearning
you can get those anywhere
cheaper too
zipped in a pocket
    étincelant
put that away or you'll lose it
so it's empty now
you wouldn't have got far

I write because I care about words and their relationship with meaning. I am attracted to poetry because, even using the most precise of tools — words and the space between them — so much of what a good poem conveys is ambiguous and indefinite.

In principle, within the limits of my poetic competence, I would like to be restrained and reticent, with (in the familiar shorthand) less being more. I am not drawn to the idea of poetry as celebration — whether of the beauty of individual words or of the truth of propositions about the world that seem obviously true.

However while one can, without contradiction, be celebratory about one's tendency to be celebratory, the same cannot be said of the opposite tendency. I am (or would like to be) suspicious of my suspicion and begrudging about my begrudgery; although less moonlights at being more, its day-job is simply being less.

So there is something of me in both voices in this poem. The voice of the italics is trying to create something but possesses only words that are flowery and clichéd. The other voice, superior and certain, is having none of it. Although this no-nonsense voice is hard to disagree with, it's not very far from 'murder your darlings' to 'kill your dreams'.

No words are plain enough to be fully transparent. In order to write anything we need to make ourselves vulnerable by choosing a set of words and arranging them on the page. Writing poetry seems to me to involve a negotiation between 'too much' and 'nothing'.

It's difficult and unforgiving but there is the grace that occasionally, in a way that seems to have very little to do with me, the words come together and reach an accommodation among themselves.

PAULA MEEHAN

The Moons

Moons like petals adrift on the stream:
night moon and day moon, moon in eclipse,
slender new moon in the winter sky,
and full harvest moon — a golden ball;
moon of my first breath, my mother's death,
grandfather moon, my father's frail boat,
moon of my lost child, my sister's fall,
moon of my beloved's waking dream,
moons of my life adrift on the stream.

What sparked this nine-line poem was a dream I had of a sky full of moons in procession, each with a direct connection to a threshold event in my life. And that sky was mirrored in a stream. I was sitting by the stream watching these events unfold and even though some of them had been traumatic in the living of them, I felt a great distance from them, and felt compassion for all who had been involved in the different dramas. I woke up happy, though I had tears on my cheeks. I felt a sense of relief and a sense of beginning. I wrote the poem down immediately on waking and forgot about it. "Time to plant tears" was a phrase ringing in my head for days after, a half line from Elizabeth Bishop's 'Sestina'.

Then I remembered some local young ones who asked me a few years back if the poem called 'Would you jump into my grave as quick?', which was on their Leaving Certificate poetry curriculum was mine. "Yes!" "We absolutely love it." "Oh thank you, I'm delighted!" "Yeah. It's lovely and short."

The poem they were referring to was only eight lines long so I began to think in terms of something shorter than a sonnet, with its impulse to argument, and something longer than a haiku, which really needs a huge charge to energise it.

Then I remembered the dream and 'The Moons'. I understood the nine-liner offered narrative possibility, though one would have to get in to the poem, resolve the material and then get out of it very quickly. I wrote a few more and before I quite realized what I was doing I was making a commemorative quilt for these commemorative years. Inspired by the commemorative quilts communities make for their young people lost to drug abuse, and quilt-making generally, I saw my endeavour as a literary equivalent, each small poem like a quilt patch using different texture, colour, patterning, together making a useful, even homely, yet still ritualised artefact. Eighty-one (9 x 9) nine-line poems, each line made up of nine syllables. I hope it is a fit expression of, and an appropriate resolution of, inherited personal and community trauma in these years of public commemoration. The sequence is called *Geomantic*. "Time to plant tears, says the almanac".

JOHN MORIARTY

Faust

Look again at your feet, Faust!
Your house smells like a stable.
The seagreen horse
And the high half hoof of stars
You saw must be conjured
Tonight from your table.

But the demons we dream of
No longer desire us
And the stakes we embraced
At our births burn out.
In the books she is Venus
In the flesh she's the virus
That holds every cell
Like a bit in its mouth.

And neighing for the beast
You must migrate through
You dream in the shade
Of the carnal tree:
Aquarius walks in the desert
Towards you;
And archangels
Grow wild at the edge of the sea.

B eing awake in the way that modern people are awake
isn't something I'm good at. After only a few years in
it, therefore, I left the modern world and came back,
happily now, to the spade and shovel I had left down.

Ivy I had planted against the wall had grown thick and strong, blinding two windows. I didn't cut it, preferring an intuitive twilight in the house. It was for the same reason that I didn't often light the lamp; even on winter nights I didn't often light it. Itself so full of shadows, there is more understanding in firelight for the kind of man I am.

Bringing water from the well and turf from the shed, these were the last two jobs I would do, darkness closing in, on a winter's evening. If the weather was hard I'd select hard sods. Cut from the deepest spit of a high bog, they were older, I'd remind myself sometimes, than Ireland's oldest folktale.

What that folktale was I didn't know, but how strange it was, crossing a yard at nightfall with a prehistoric landscape in a bag on my back. For the rest of the night I would sit prehistorically by the fire and life and light of it. That suited me. There was something I was good at. It came naturally to me on winter nights to sink to the sod's level.

It came naturally to me, sitting there, to sink into the deepest spit of mind in me. And that was a dreaming spit, dreaming its dream with a hawthorn bush, dreaming their dreams with mountain and star.

When I came to live in Connemara in the 1980s I felt an immediate affinity with the natural world, felt I had come home to myself too in a strange way. I would sit for hours at a time, next to a whitethorn tree perhaps, letting it work on what I would call my bush soul. This type of contemplation has always been central to my way of thinking.

It brought me back to the bog world of North Kerry, the Leitrim Hill of my youth, the child world where communion with nature was entirely possible and within reach.

I withdrew from what I would call the material world, the bustling campus of McMaster university in Manitoba where I was teaching, to engage with the natural world, an immersion that brought me on an intuitive journey that shaped itself into a book called *Dreamtime*.

I believe we are intrinsically and umbilically connected with everything on earth; trees have veins and need to feed just like ourselves. My project has its roots in ancient myth but also in the Christian mystics, St. Francis and John of the Cross.

Dreamtime surprised people — some called it an Irish Upanishad. I've always seen it as an entirely natural extension of the Aisling tradition, mystical poems where the poet allows himself to be dreamed by a myth rather than controlling the process.

It's about the humility of surrender, knowing our place in the world, admitting that radical new forms of thinking and of engagement with the natural world are needed if we are to survive as a species.

AIDAN MURPHY

Touching Parallels

All night I dug for a reasonable word,
a perfect verse handknit from salvage,
a poem you might wear on a cold night.
Now my notebook bulges with atrocity,
the diary of a sick, unfeeling species.

I want him on the line.
My guilt wants to parley with his.
My mouth wants to sing in his ear.
I dial. The phone rings ...

Who'll deny this is a wicked moment
but there is no other; this fact assists
my breathing down the deaf shell. (He's
in the shower, a wet towel trails
across the tiles. Caked with soap
his hand is closing in on the receiver,

and it freezes there. The instrument
silent in its cradle.) Clients queue
outside, waving coins, itching
to pile into these upright tombs
for shots of hope. It's a poor service,
most will fail,
                    strangled by ruthless tapes,
                    shamed by cybernetic language,
                    doublecrossed by gadgetry that
                    never weakens or desires.

'Touching Parallels' was written in the late 1970s and it appeared in my first poetry collection *The Restless Factor* which was published by Raven Arts Press / Colin Smythe Ltd. in 1985. The poem is best read and understood if located in that time period, which was long before the arrival of the answering machine, the voicemail, the email, the internet etc … which would make the premise of not connecting with someone immediately somewhat redundant.

However, though the pressing of button A and B and the heavy black dial telephones are part of our history now, it is relevant that such artefacts of the past are preserved in writing.

Themes touched upon within the poem resurface throughout my later work, right up to the present. The limitations of language, a sense of urban isolation and paranoia, the complexities involved in attempting to communicate oneself to another, the gulf that can exist between even the closest of friends and lovers, human frailty versus harsh mechanical realities.

It has, I think, a solid visual quality that reflects my passion for the cinema, and the use of cinema technique as a poetic device gets a little play here. The cutting between the caller and the called (the called, alas, arriving too late to pick up the receiver) akin to a split screen in a movie.

There are also, I hope, hints of sexual ambiguity and mystery. What is it that the person dialling wishes to tell the other? Why the desperation, the urgency? Why the mention of guilt? Is it love? Is it a matter of life and death?

GERRY MURPHY

Poem in One Breath

Not that you
would notice
but every time
you pass
up the corridor
Lenin's statue
levitates slightly
to get a better view
of the remarkable ease
with which you fill
curved space.

This poem first saw the publishing light in *Quarryman* in 1983. It was written in 1981 while I was living in a bedsit on Wellington Road [Cork] mere yards away from the poets Thomas McCarthy and Seán Dunne. It was inspired by Cathy O'Rourke, a teacher who visited the pool where I had recently started working. I remember knowing I had to write something to celebrate her captivating beauty but with no idea where to start.

I was as surprised by the finished poem as anyone. In fact it went on for two or three lines more and only in re-reading it the next morning did I see its natural ending.

It was the first poem of mine to stir a response in my small circle of readers, and not all of it positive. I sent it to *New Irish Writing* twice, thinking David Marcus was insane to reject it the first time. He rejected it the second time as well. It eventually became the opening poem in my first collection *A Small Fat Boy Walking Backwards*. It has remained a favourite poem of mine over the years; on request I once read it from the flagpole in the square in Carrignavar at a student party in 1984.

I think it is a synopsis of my attitude to love and politics, serious issues but not to be taken too seriously. Here in the poem they co-exist happily in thirty-two words.

MADELAINE NERSON Mac NAMARA

Atlas

What the eyes weigh in thin daylight
scales the atlas of sleeping hours
what bathes the ears of clean sunrise
towels fresh tunes to dance in dreams.

What the skin tastes at dark noontime
robes long echoes of cliff and tide
what the tongue reads in salt or ice
tosses a fig at hill lightning.

What jasmine breathes in mirage heat
frescoes the cell of moonless night
what planets track across dawn skies
is the wingspan of abrupt joy.

What trees demand in silent dusk
is the wild right to stand neighbours
what winds retrace in cloud and mist
is the ungrieved shape of mountains.

What storms reckon at equinox
is the balance of ledge and nest
what meets waters of rain and sea
is the shelter of sister shores.

What rainbows pluck from narrow air
frees the colour of plain chant flowers
what heartstrings draw from even ground
is a reason for volcanoes.

What scorch of sand tells running child
is that surprise weaves and throws pots
what swishing weeds whisper temples
is the ocean's fond remembering.

What mud calls out to young sailors
weighing on oars is wait for me
what blueberries decipher last
is the riddle of waterfalls.

'Atlas' brings together impressions and images gathered mostly during my own life, and some through hearsay or books. They had been so intensely experienced, so securely stored in memory that they stubbornly refused to be forgotten, kept bubbling up, impatient to be acknowledged, given a place in some or other scheme of things.

I remember an afternoon's drive in childhood, me, like my young brother, sitting propped up on a few Harrap's dictionaries, my parents in front, often singing together, 'Green Sleeves' a great favourite.

In between songs they would chat, sometimes comment on the landscape, which was the countryside of Île de France, west of Paris. Some of it much changed since they had last seen it, before World War II. But it was unchanged in the area we were now traversing, a rolling, open land, mostly undulating fields of ripe wheat, chequered with hay meadows.

My mother turned back towards me and invited me to observe how beautiful it was, my father concurring. I remember looking at the immense fields, seeing them as if for the first time, finding myself agreeing fully with my parents, realising I had never thought of, nor noticed beauty before.

I seemed to know with certainty that from now on I would look for it as often as I could, quite trusting that it would present itself to be seen. In a moment the world had become a much more interesting place.

A few years later, around age ten or eleven, I discovered the world wasn't perfect, nor was I myself. And so 'Atlas', attempting to honour these two strands of perception, these two world views, is perhaps both lament for a messy, cruel world, and celebration of the same beautiful, mysterious and against all odds and appearances, hopeful world.

CAITRÍONA NÍ CHLÉIRCHÍN

Feiliceán bán

D'éalaigh feiliceán bán
ó do bhéal an lá gur éag tú
is i dtaibhreamh buan
i dtromshuan atá tú ó shin

ar fán in aisling shíoraí,
schmetterling ar eití ime
dealán de nó papillon blanc
mariposa, memento mori, peidhleacán

Peidhleacán Persephone marbh anois
nach ann di anois ach aer
gile is éadroime, tú imithe as
saor sa saol eile — i do pheidhleacan solais

claochlú nó ceileatram
bánóg i measc na lilí,
nóiméad ciúnais, glór sagairt, cleitearnach
brothall sochraide, cré, scamall trín ghriain

Princeam agus eiteall an fheiliceáin
mionchraitheadh sciathán
diamhair i mbreacsholas an tráthnóna
mí Iúil na Súl buí sa chroí, taobh an uaigh

Imíonn feiliceán bán isteach
san áit a raibh do ghormrosc
istigh i do bhlaosc, faoin fholt óir
is aniar arís as do bhéal

i móinéar na mbrionglóidí.

White Butterfly

A white butterfly
escaped your mouth
the day you died
it fluttered forth
A timeless dream
An everlasting sleep

Wandering ever since,
Soft-winged Schmetterling,
You are my wisp-like papillon
My Mariposa and memento mori,
My eternal butterfly-dream

You are the Persephone's Butterfly
That vanished
And all that is left is air
A bright butterfly
Light as disappearance
The freedom
Of the other realm

Did you exchange yourself for
Someone else?
A fresh veneer of yourself
Are you a bawnogue amongst the lilies,
Did I hear you flutter
In a silent moment
Or a priest's words
In the heavy funereal silence
I hear the heft of earth
The sun breaking through

Are you there still
Aside the grave
In the quiet flicker of
butterfly wings
Or the furtive half-light
Of July's yellow butter-heart

The day you died
A white butterfly
Fluttered free
Across the eternal meadow
It flew into the shell of yourself
Disappeared beneath the golden hair of your dreaming
It became as one
With your everlasting blue

Translation by Mícheál Ó hAodha

I wrote this poem, 'Feileacán bán' (published in *Comhar*, February 2016, not as yet collected, and translated kindly here by Mícheál Ó hAodha as 'White Butterfly'), in memory of my late mother. It was almost a year and a half after she died that I was able to write this poem about seeing a white butterfly at her burial in July 2014. My mother suffered a long battle with the terrible illness called emphysema and I watched her struggle to breathe and slowly deteriorate before my eyes in hospital and in the nursing home for four years. During this time I was haunted by many signs and premonitions and wrote poems about these also. Some of the symbols of death were more comforting such as 'Capall bán'/ 'White Horse' collected in *Coiscéim An Bhrídeach Sí* (2014), but some were ominous.

The white butterfly can be seen as the eternal soul of a loved one who has just passed away. After my mother died, whenever I saw a white butterfly, I felt a sense of comfort and her spiritual presence in the lonely and painful time of her grief, and I could feel a sense of her release from the pain of her illness.

I was also inspired by a passage in Muiris Ó Suilleabháin's *Fiche Bliain ag Fás* about a white butterfly journeying during a dream from the mouth of a young boy, down a meadow and in and out of a horse's skull and back up the meadow and into the boy's mouth again when he stopped dreaming. I was at the time teaching a course in the University of Limerick on the Blasket Island Literature. There is an ethereal quality to the butterfly episode, deriving I think from local folklore.

I started thinking also about Persephone and her butterfly and all the different names for butterfly in French, German and Spanish and how beautiful those names were. I would say that there is a contrast in the poem between the magical surrealism — the beauty of my mother's blue eyes and blonde hair, and the butterfly and the sun — and the stark and harsh reality of death, decay and the skull and her dead body beneath the clay. It took me a long time to write this poem and release it from my soul, and when I did I felt a mixture of happiness and extreme sorrow, thinking of all the grief that it cost.

NUALA NÍ CHONCHÚIR

Tatú

Is pailmseist mo chorp
faoi do lámha,
paipír ársa
scrollaithe fút,
ag tnúth le do rian.
Glanaim mo chraiceann,
sciúraim siar é
go pár báiteach
ionas go bpúchfaidh
do lámh mar
dhúch tatuála,
ag líníocht thar
línte dofheicthe
gach fir eile.

Níl faic ach tusa
scrábáilte ar mo chorp.

Tattoo

My body is a palimpsest
under your hands,
a papyrus scroll
unfurled beneath you,
waiting for your mark.
I clean my skin,
scrape it back to
a pale parchment,
so that your touch
can sink as deep

as the tattooist's ink,
and leave its tracery
over the erased lines
of other men.

You are all that's
written on my body.

'Tatú' was written on a day of deep sorrow. I had put an end to a relationship — there were too many impossibilities. I was heartsore, wrung-out, defeated. And still in love. I wrote the poem in one gulp. It entertains me now that I used the present tense in the poem, which suggests I wasn't as finished with this lover as I imagined when I cried a Liffey of tears and wrote. Surely the past tense would have been the more permanent choice?

The word *'pailmseist'* makes the first line sing, I think. I had recently done a reading with the poet Ian Duhig who had read from *The Lammas Hireling*. In that collection there is a poem called 'Blood', about the joys of a teenage boy's self-adornment, that talks about a pair of oxblood Oxfords as 'Chippendale-varnish palimpsests of spit and polish'. 'Palimpsest' floated like a feather at that reading and landed in my lap — it reminded me of things I had studied at university, about Irish monks and their manuscripts. And I loved the raspy sound of the word and the fact that it is on the cusp of being difficult to say. So I took 'palimpsest' and stored it, as writers do, and soon it emerged in 'Tatú'.

What amazes me now, re-reading Ian's poem, is that it is also about the boy planning a tattoo on the 'unilluminated manuscript' of his body. Ha! I had recently had my first tattoo. And 'The Lammas Hireling' was a present from The Lover. So I see now that I took more than a word from Ian's poem, I took an idea — the body as parchment — and moved away with it to write about something deeply personal.

Reader, that same lover is *still* all that's written on my body.

EILÉAN NÍ CHUILLEANÁIN

The Copious Dark

She used to love the darkness, how it brought
Closer the presence of flesh, the white arms and breast
Of a stranger in a railway carriage a dim glow —
Or the time when the bus drew up at a woodland corner
And a young black man jumped off, and a shade
Moved among shades to embrace him under the leaves —

Every frame of a lit window, the secrets bared —
Books packed warm on a wall — each blank shining blind,
Each folded hush of shutters without a glimmer,
Even the sucked-sweet tones of neon reflected in rain
In insomniac towns, boulevards where the odd light step
Was a man walking alone: they would all be kept,

Those promises, for people not yet in sight:
Wellsprings she still kept searching for after the night
When every wall turned yellow. Questing she roamed
After the windows she loved, and again they showed
The back rooms of bakeries, the clean engine-rooms and all
The floodlit open yards where a van idled by a wall,

A wall as long as life, as long as work.
                                 The blighted
Shuttered doors in the wall are too many to scan —
As many as the horses in the royal stable, as the lighted
Candles in the grand procession? Who can explain
Why the wasps are asleep in the dark in their numbered holes
And the lights shine all night in the hospital corridors?

I suppose the poems that appeal most to us as writers are the ones that seem to have solved big creative problems. In my case the problem that haunted me for decades was how to deal with negative feelings, with UNeasiness, UNfairness. Negative words sometimes have a fine polysyllabic rattle, but they give the reader no hints to construct an imaginary journey with. They can relieve the writer's feelings but they do not show a way out of the cul-de-sac.

Another preoccupation: since childhood I had wanted to write about a child's fear of big institutional buildings, hospitals, factories, schools. I've had to learn to manage those fears as an adult, but a layer of anxiety persists, and erupts when I pass a long long factory whose windows cannot be counted, whose loading bays and parked vans seem to stretch my idea of human scale until it hurts. Or I drive under a huge motorway arch, the road sweeping grandly, carrying me off without resistance, and I spot them on a stony verge, a little bunch of men with small bags, waiting for a lorry to bring them to exploitative work. It is not quite day, the yellow lamplight sharpens their shadows.

Once I was on a bus on winding roads in Virginia and I saw a lovely black girl waiting in dusk where the bus stopped, and the embrace when her lover got off. That gave me the idea of writing about darkness, nightfall, as the natural element of home and closeness, as opposed to the smooth persistence of artificial light. This is, underneath, a poem about the great unfairness of work, between men and women, men exiled from their families when their bodily strength is wanted by the machine, women left raising children alone and surviving on miserable part-time wages. The feeling in the poem comes from those two moments of looking at men.

AILBHE NÍ GHEARBHUIGH

Deireadh na Feide

Inniu féin
is cuimhin le muintir Aas
go mbíodh teanga
á feadaíl
ages na haoirí
fadó,

fead a ghabh
bealach fuaime an ghleanna
idir féarach is sráidbhaile,

fead a d'iompair
nuacht an lae
idir aoirí
agus na mná a d'oibrigh
sna goirt máguaird,

feadaíl nach dtuigtí
lasmuigh den bparóiste.

Nuair a tháinig na Naitsithe
choimeád an feadaíl
Giúdaigh slán ó chontúirt;
chuir scéalta an *Résistance*
ó bhéal go béal faoi rún;
chabhraigh le píolótaí 'bhí imithe amú
teorainn na Spáinne a aimsiú.

Níor chualathas ó shin í.

Maireann sí i gcuimhne na ndaoine,
an teanga feadaíola seo,
ach níl ar chumas éinne
na fuaimeanna a aithris.

Níor deineadh aon taifead.

Last Blast

Even now
the people of Aas can remember
the long-ago whistling
language
of shepherds,

whistles that followed
the acoustic echoey channel
from village to pasture,

whistles that carried
the day's tittle-tattle
between herdsmen
and the women of the homesteads,

whistles not understood
beyond the limits of their parish.

When the Nazis invaded
the whistling-tongue kept
Jews from coming to harm;
it passed resistance messages,
secretly, from lip to pursed lip,
and helped crashed allied pilots
reach the border with Spain.

It hasn't been heard since.

It has a half-life, this whistling language,
in the memories of certain parishioners
but none now are capable
of producing the sounds.

It was never recorded.

Translated by Billy Ramsell

I*s fánach an áit a bhfaighfeá gliomach.* You might find a lobster in the queerest of places. Mired in the thick of my doctoral research, a book was recommended to me by a colleague called *The Discovery of France* by Graham Robb. Neither an academic book, nor strictly related to my research topic, I was somewhat perplexed. Reading had ceased to be a pleasurable activity by this point: books and scholarly articles were mined for information; arguments were gleaned and stockpiled for future use. Everything must have a function.

Poems weren't coming easily to me at this time and what I did manage to write lacked dexterity and punch. In the years since publishing my first book, *Péacadh* (2008), I had developed a better idea about what I wanted my poems to achieve. I just wasn't there yet.

In *The Discovery of France*, I came across a short anecdote about a whistling language that once existed in the Pyrenees. It was likely a source of bemusement or even derision for the Parisian visitor — these 'peasants' communicating like birds. It was, however, quite a sophisticated means of communication that could travel great distances across valleys and convey a lot of information. During the Second World War, this shepherd-language would become vital for the survival of Jews who were fleeing Occupied France.

Thus began an obsession with marginalized languages, with unusual modes of communication, with how we relate to each other despite our flawed instruments of expression. These ideas are central to the poems in *Tost agus Allagar* (2016). I was particularly interested in those peripheral or obsolete languages that had a purpose — a subconscious response, perhaps, to those external voices who question the 'usefulness' of the Irish language. Everything does have a function.

Tú Féin is Mé Féin

Thógamar teach féir — tú féin is mé féin — ag
bun an mhóinéir. Do thrí scór bliain dod chromadh
ach fós bhí na ballaí chomh hard liom féin.

Chnag tú ar chloch an dorais. Bhuail isteach.
'Mise Daidí, tusa Mam,' a dúirt go séimh, 'is mé
ag filleadh ort tar éis obair an lae.' D'ólamar
tae as cupáin bheaga bhréige.

'Téanam ort, a chroí. Tá sé in am luí. Bain
díot.' Is bhain. Bhain tú piliúr as balla na
cistine. Do thrí scór bliain dom phlúchadh.

D'éiríomar. Ghlan le do chiarsúr mé. Phóg mo
chuid fola leis an gcréacht a leigheas is
d'fhilleamar — tú féin is mé féin — ar theach
mo mháthar, ar theach d'iníne.

Ach pé sracfhéachaint a thugaim thar mo ghuaille
feicim fós ó am go chéile an chréacht oscailte
a d'fhág tú i mballa na cistine.

Yourself and Myself

We built a grass house — yourself and myself — at
the foot of the meadow. You — hunched under your
three score years. Me — no higher than the walls.

You knocked on our stone door. Came in.
'I'll be the Daddy, you be Mam,' you said softly,
'and I'll be coming home from my day's work,'
We drank tea out of toy cups.

'Come on, my love. It's time for bed. Strip off.'
I stripped. You plucked a pillow from the kitchen
wall. Your three score years suffocated me.

You cleaned me with your handkerchief. Kissed
my blood to heal the wound and we walked home
— yourself and myself — to the house of my
mother, your daughter.

Sometimes when I glance over my shoulder
I still see the gaping wound you left
in the kitchen wall.

Translated by Pádraig Ó Snodaigh

This poem grew out of an idea for a radio series.
In the early 1990s, I spent a few years commuting as a
freelance journalist between London and Dublin. In the
course of my work on a radio series on the Irish in London,
I came across a number of people who had left Ireland many
years earlier but were still carrying the scars of the physical and
sexual abuse they had suffered as children.

Back in Dublin for a few days, I had a meeting with the late
radio producer, Peter Mooney. Following a long discussion, he
and I began researching a possible series of radio programmes
on child sexual abuse. We made sample recordings with
counsellors and survivors of abuse in both Ireland and
England. Several months later, we submitted a proposal to RTÉ

— together with a selection of these sample recordings. The proposal was rejected — for 'legal reasons'. The 'powers that were' believed that there could be legal repercussions if voices were recognised.

I listened again and again to the recordings and was haunted by images and stories. I have always had a passion for giving a voice to those who — for one reason or another — have lost or have been deprived of the ability to speak out. I gradually began to weave the images into poems.

Many of these poems (including this one) were published by Dedalus/Coiscéim in *Deora Nár Caoineadh / Unshed Tears* (1996).

DOIREANN NÍ GHRÍOFA

From Richmond Hill

Home from hospital, you doze in my arms, milk-drunk,
all eyelashes, cheeks and raw umbilical, swaddled
in the heavy black smell of the brewery.

Your great-grandfathers worked all their lives in that factory.
Every day they were there, breathing the same air, hoisting
barrels, sweating over vats where black bubbles rose like fat.

At dusk, they poured into pubs, and ordered porter,
neat black pints lidded with white silk, thick as cream
from frothing milk, and their replies were always the same:

the gasp, the nod. Down gullets and guts went the porter,
went the pay, went the nights and days. Every day
the same — coins slapped on the counter. No change.

In my arms, you stir. A thousand streetlamps
flicker to light in the dusk. As I watch your eyes open,
the reek of roasting hops knits a blanket of scent around us.

N*ow: a morning in late January in a sun-filled kitchen. My baby daughter gurgles and giggles in her highchair, her chubby fingers feeling for rice-cakes and chunks of banana that she has already tossed over the edge. I sip tea and wonder over words like 'seminal' and 'oeuvre'.*

Today marks six years from when I wrote my very first poem. Only six years, although it feels like much longer. How can I understand, at such an early juncture in my writing life, what is or what will become seminal to my work? I can only guess. With that in mind, I choose a poem in which I sense some recurrent motifs of mine, ideas that my writing mind is helpless before: the palimpsest of past and present, generational inheritance, pregnancy and childbirth. The poem 'From Richmond Hill' still tingles with a sort of static electricity for me. When I wrote it, we lived in a tiny hillside house in Cork city, four of us in a narrow terraced house, a two-up, two-down. I often sat at the window, looking out at the city glittering and squirming in the valley below. That particular gaze has become mythic in my writing, and although we moved elsewhere some years ago, many of my poems still breathe in that space. 'From Richmond Hill' is emblematic of a time, a way of thinking that recurs in my work. At that time, I was oblivious to how significant it would become for me. We can never know what will become pivotal in our work, or in our lives for that matter. We can only write what we must.

Now: I wipe the table, gather the dishes. Steam rises from my empty cup.

MARY NOONAN

The Moths

The artist is sitting, perfectly still,
by his mulberry tree, watching
it. He has been in that pose all day.

The white moths have flown
through my open window,
drawn by the light of a bedside lamp.

They are everywhere — cloaking
the walls, sleeping in the folds of sheets,
crawling over the shoes on the floor.

I try to flatten some with newspaper
but they are too many, and I lie down
among them. Soon, they cover me,

their anaemic wings lining the creases
of my eyelids, lashes thrumming
to the sound of a thousand tiny wings

flicking. In the bed, I rustle. Moths are
spinning from hairs, slinking over the skin
of my scalp and pubis. I lie in a rictus.

In the morning, I walk on a flittered
bridal veil of wings, from bed to bathroom.
I pass the artist. He is sitting

by the fish tank, watching his black
piranha slip through cool water,
behind glass. Has he been there all night?

'The Moths' was written after a short stay in a place where I felt very uncomfortable. My discomfort was more psychic than physical, and yet the moths were real — they really were there, as described in the poem.

The poem, therefore, came out of a desire to release some of the lingering feelings the place and its occupant had given me. And the metaphor was to hand. This was lucky, as metaphors are not always so available, so ready to oblige by fitting the feeling so aptly. So, I was guided by the metaphor, and some pent-up stress.

The tercet is an unusual form for me, and the lines are shorter than my lines would usually be. I think this form came out of a desire to communicate a sense of enclosure or entrapment. The artist-figure book-ending the poem also contributes to the sense of sequestration. The artist is a model of cold and inscrutable stasis, while almost everything in-between is a hot-bed of riotous activity.

Although I can trace a stimulus that may have triggered the poem, it seemed to come, more or less formed, from my unconscious, in that it evokes feelings and ideas which I did not consciously intend. A reader subsequently said there was something erotic going on, though I had no sense of this when writing it.

Moths are ancient symbols of death, of the soul or psyche, and also of metamorphosis. I didn't make the connection between the mulberry tree and the moths until long after the poem was written, but of course silk worms feed off the leaves of the mulberry tree until they pupate into moths.

This links the tree with the moth and silk, which makes a link to the bridal gown implied by the bridal veil, perhaps.

Why is this poem a touchstone for me? Because I'd love all poems to come to me in this way. The strong metaphor arrives as a gift — a crucible within which the poem comes to be. The metaphor channels the feelings and ideas the poet feels she must convey.

Yet the finished poem reveals that the unconscious had other plans for the poem, and that it's doing something quite other than what the writer had originally intended.

JULIE O'CALLAGHAN

Edible Anecdote #6

I drove out to the Casa del Sol shopping center
with the kids this morning
and in between the times when one of them
was grabbing bags of Hershey's Kisses
and insisting I buy them
and the other was poking his mitten
in the live lobster tank
I became depressed
and clutched something to renew my spirits:
Frozen Chocolate Cream Pie

Edible Anecdote #17

oh yeah, it's an all-you-can-eat
salad buffet alright
but did you notice that your rear-end
barely fits on these chairs
and to get past the other tables
you have to hold your breath?
not only that, but every time you get up
with your plate you're surrounded my mirrors
telling you that your spare tire
and midriff bulge are thriving
and that everyone in the place
is watching your blubber ripple
to top it all off the waitresses are thing as sticks
oh yeah, all-you-can-eat my eye

RECIPE FOR EDIBLE ANECDOTES

It was the mid to late 1970s and Dennis O'Driscoll and I were sharing a flat in Dublin. I had gotten over my initial mild annoyance of living with someone who knew more about my poems than I did and was happily working away on what I thought of as my homesick-for-Chicago poems. I would show small groups of them to Dennis every once in a while and he would mark them up — very like a teacher in school — and I would make the 'corrections' and keep going. I was having myself a wonderful boo-hoo-fest thinking them up.

At some stage he said: *OK, show me all of the poems you've been working on.* I gathered-up the poems and we spread them out. Now the torture began. He lifted each piece of paper and read it. If I nervously started trying to explain or justify or comment on any of them as he read them he would say — how can I read and talk at the same time? So I sat there silently waiting for the verdict. He was making two piles of papers: some would go in one pile and some would go in the other. I had no idea what the piles meant.

Then came the pronouncement: *The poems in this pile are very good. But they are NOT poems about Chicago or poems about being homesick.* I was like — what?? That's what I was working on — poems that reminded me of Chicago! *They are poems on one topic — FOOD AND EATING.* I was stunned. I grabbed the papers and began to read. GOOD GOD! They were poems about eating and food. Until that moment I had no idea what I was even writing about!

The second pile of papers were scraps for the garbage can.

Doubting Thomas

Whoever or whatever, since we might be here
By chance, ordained that we come to life
Also ordained that we grow tired of wonders.
The visionaries at Knock went for supper
Knowing that the vision would not last.
Or the day I myself took a breather from
A once in a lifetime sighting of an otter
Showing itself in a gully miles upstream
From the river where it had been born.
Knowing that the vision would not last
Until I got back, that however I embellished
The story for the sceptic in the pub, nothing
Would compensate for the finger in the wound,
The shock at the eyes in the head of the being.

'Doubting Thomas' clarifies a few things for me. The 'otherness' of the creature — an otter that appears during a hill walk in an isolated valley — shocks me into a realisation of an 'otherness', a deeper dimension to our life than received wisdom would have us believe.

'The shock at the eyes in the head of the being' woke me to something in my Self — surely a poem must clarify something for the poet if it is to have meaning for a reader.

A poem, to my mind, that justifies its existence and my own vocation as a poet: those long years of reflection, of 'looking into the abyss'. A meditation, I like to think, on Wonder — that word appropriated, often shamelessly, by commerce to flog its wares. A word that belongs, surely, to the realm of Art, that allows us to reflect on the 'otherness' of our human experience.

'Doubting Thomas, the alter ego of the poem, mirrors a scepticism in my own nature, the wear and tear on the psyche of years at the Poetic Coalface, but also an optimism, an openness to new experience — 'wonder' at the ability of art to transform that experience.

It clarifies aspects of my own personality, an ascetic sensibility drawn to the natural world, an irreverent streak. I like to think that the native religious iconography (Knock) that the poem references, the lore of a particular place *(dinnsenchas)*, counters the fashion among a certain caste of poets, if I may use that term, to reference classical motifs as if our own mythologies and traditions were somehow less worthy.

The search for Identity is at the heart of this poem and, I suspect, at the heart of all our enterprises, the need to justify our existence, to make our lives significant. 'The shock at the eyes in the head of the being' is a reflection on my own self — reflects something of that Self, hopefully, for the reader.

JOHN O'DONNELL

The Shipping Forecast

for my father

Tied up at the pier in darkened harbour
the two of us below, in cabin's amber
light; me surly in a sleeping-bag, fifteen,
and you, past midnight, calmly tuning in
to the Shipping Forecast, Long Wave's
crackle, hiss, until you find the voice.
What's next for us: rain or fair? There are
warnings of gales in Rockall and Finisterre.
So near now, just this teak bulkhead
between us, and yet so apart, battened
hatches as another low approaches, the high
over Azores as distant as a man is from a boy.
I think of my own boat one day, the deep.
Beside me the sea snores, turns over in its sleep.

Like prospectors, poets are always anxious to know if what they've unearthed this time is the real thing. We make our marks and see how they compare; and there are so many other marks already, from others who for centuries have been panning for gold in the same seam.

Some poems, we know, are no more than fool's gold, their brassy yellow quickly losing its glister, though sadly not always before they've made their way into print; it's often difficult at the time of writing to tell.

It was Touchstone himself who said "the truest poetry is the most feigning", in *As You Like It,* and, as a clown, he should know, planted as he is by Shakespeare to call things as they are rather than as we might like them to be. He would make a useful editor, standing at our shoulders as we write; mostly shaking his head sadly, but occasionally — very occasionally — crying' Yes!'

I've chosen 'The Shipping Forecast' from my first collection *Some Other Country* as my touchstone poem because, although it was written nearly twenty years ago, it's a poem that still makes me say "Yes". It combines, in the sonnet form I love, many of the themes I've returned to often, the struggle to grow up, the father-son relationship, and the sea.

John F. Kennedy suggested we all have in our veins "the exact same percentage of salt in our blood that exists in the ocean, and, therefore, we have salt in our blood, in our sweat, in our tears". I'm sure there are scientists who disagree. But like a lot of what Kennedy said, it *feels* right, as I hope this poem does; and if someone years from now sifting through my poems stop at this one, I hope they'll agree.

MARY O'DONNELL

The World is Mine

July 1, 2014

From Antrim to Wexford, the sun steals
over the shore's grey hem. It is July,
and people wake to their worlds

in old Viking towns, on estuaries,
in the bright estates that curve like
spines on the edges of towns.

Here is the pace of a summer morning:
a lone walker with dogs on a beach,
new light pouring into the hollows of shells,

along the slow glint of dunes where grasses
dip sculptural and silver. What I want is to know
that this can continue, that other mornings

I remember as folds and bolts
of light, the shouting and crosshatch
of bird annunciations, the rustle

of small animals as they move back
for another day in a burrow's darkness,
will stay safe. Is it a question of time?

The atmosphere is thinner, earth threadbare
from a steady weave of hands and neurons
as we make space for millions, while icecaps

melt and deserts spread like spilled ochre.
This morning, those yellows fall moistly
on the shorelines, light has pushed

across hills, through the tillage-acred fields
of Kildare, flashing the duns and greys of horses
riding out at the Curragh's long acres,

on, on to the bog's wild cottons,
stirring larks, a lone heron holding taut
in a meditation of water, a flash of young trout.

Finally, the Shannon is lit, cataracts and bubbles
brighten through the West and its days
of shifting emigrants, students, hopes

of dolphins drawing them home as if to healing.
From Antrim to Wexford, sun has spilt
across the sleeping island, till Galway, Limerick

steady themselves into full colour, as I once
steadied myself when I was ten and watched
an orchard brightening, seized my day.

And now. Another July.
We are waking and working to our worlds,
what is known and unknown,
the world still mine.

I n summer 1967 our family holidayed in south Co. Wexford,
in a rambling castle hotel. It had turret rooms and all the
romantic trappings of ancientness that appealed to my
thirteen-year-old imagination. One afternoon I slipped away

into a small wood. It was dark and lovely, and it echoed with the sound of thrushes and blackbirds.

I lay down on the grass with my book, but couldn't read. But I did have a pencil and I wrote my first-ever poem there and then. An exciting yet serene sense of being a sole discoverer, of having stumbled into a special, very green, dimension, overcame me.

It wasn't the first time I had had this experience. And by now I knew that an authority was conferred on me by simply knowing this place, this sanctuary, my kingdom: it was the authority of transcendence.

Later, where else could I speak of my deep excitement, my profound gratitude at the beauty of the world except through poetry? Who would hear me? So there's a twist in my personality which finds me always slightly primed for the possibility of primal innocence, which can be found only in the natural world, with its lucencies, patterns and rhythms. 'The World is Mine', written in 2014, has become a touchstone poem which speaks to a poetic and personal need for — perhaps — rapture.

I got up much earlier than usual on the first of July. Because of that, I was able to celebrate the arrival of the sun, sensing its gradual journey across the whole of Ireland, filling darkness with light and chill with warmth. The poem also, towards the end, speaks to a time in my youth when I was totally enchanted by beauty in the place I grew up, and watched an orchard brighten into the floral pinks of dawn.

I'm glad I was able to pay attention to such things. It made a poet of me, because poets must pay attention.

BERNARD O'DONOGHUE

The Iron Age Boat at Caumatruish

If you doubt, you can put your fingers
In the holes where the oar-pegs went.
If you doubt still, look past its deep mooring
To the mountains that enfold the corrie's
Waterfall of lace through which, they say,
You can see out but not in.
If you doubt that, hear the falcon
Crying down from Gneeves Bog
Cut from the mountain-top. And if you doubt
After all these witnesses, no boat
Dredged back from the dead
Could make you believe.

Caumatruish (or Coomeenatruish, in a slightly less anglicised version) is a townland a few miles to the south of Millstreet in North Cork, behind Kilmedey Castle and overshadowed by Clara Mountain. There is a small lake there at the foot of a waterfall that flows down from the bleak expanse of Gneeves Bog on the mountainside. Some time in the 1960s the farmer who owns the land around the lake, Thade Mullane, was dredging the land by the lakeside and the machine scooped up a log boat which had been preserved by the bog-water. Thade stopped operations straightaway to protect the remarkable survivor from two millennia back. He kept the boat in peace in a gully, just beneath the surface of the brackish water that still preserves it. I visited it first in the late 1980s. Like everyone else I was made very welcome by Thade Mullane who left the access open through his farmyard for visitors there. You might call them pilgrims.

The theme of the poem I suppose is faith and doubt, put in

the context of two New Testament stories. The first is the story of Doubting Thomas who said he would not believe Christ was risen from the dead until he had put his fingers in the wounds in his hands. The second is the story of Dives and Lazarus, the rich man and the poor leper. Dives dies and is condemned to Hell for his indulgent life. He — rather unselfishly — asks God to send Lazarus down from Heaven to warn Dives's brothers about their eternal fate. But he is told that, if people on earth will not believe the saints and the prophets, they will not believe someone who returns from the dead.

So the poem says that, in beautiful places like this, we have plenty of evidence to have faith in the worth and beauty of the world. And, as a footnote, Thade Mullane was a kind of saint who was always proud and grateful that the boat was on his land as a visitant sent from another, higher realm.

LIZ O'DONOGHUE

Suspended Animation

There may as well
be a galaxy between us
you on some remote star
and me adrift.

Solitary
contemplating a screen
through swirls of cosmic dust
until my eyes water.

I follow the beam between moons
nausea's got my appetite
weightlessness
makes me wane.

Splendid visions
of your mountainous landscape
flash intermittently
until I am shocked
out of senselessness
by the sharpening cold …

this interminable space
is cold, silent and cold
the dogs and bears are silent
silence between the sheets
silence between my lips
silence in vast swathes
of emptiness
vast interminable silence.

Where are you?

Skysign with the tail of a comet.
Rearrange the stars as an arrow.
Bounce a signal off Saturn.

Time floats like a mist
and I'm suspended within …
its eerie faint groan
excising another hour from our lives
days and nights
drag each other from their beds
fighting for the last shred of light.

The screen is dead
this craft won't spark
the outer casing is dented
the log has run out of days.

The space between us
is only physical
my hand even now
is in yours.

Silence is replaced
with the quietness
of skin on skin.

I was born into the Space Age and I remember distinctly in 1969 at the age of eight having nightmares about being cut off from a spaceship and drifting eternally in a vacuum. The world was filled with Neil Armstrong and his mission to the moon.

I remember, even at that age, grappling with the idea of infinity. I remember my mother getting me out of bed to watch the moon landing live — just me, none of my siblings. I was old enough to grasp the enormity of what was happening.

This poem echoes the nightmare. This poem encapsulates my search for the elusive planet of deep, reciprocal love. I have ever been adrift and never found it. It was written because I hadn't heard from someone I'd fallen head-over-heels for, in six weeks.

Just as I'd thought he was genuinely interested I began to think he'd changed his mind. I was lost in deep anxiety.

Much of my life's been lived in chaos as I've counted it in unrequited loves and loves I have spurned and in the maelstroms, the dark matter; live a deafening silence and no one to call home.

MARY O'DONOGHUE

My Daughter in Winter Costume

after John Storr's sculpture (1922)

She is sealed like a bomb in her anorak.
Her face is flushed fruit under the hood.
She's already moving away. I want to call her back.

At nine in the morning the sky is blue-black.
I think of hard falls, split lips, her blood.
But she's sealed like a bomb in her anorak,

and shouting to friends on the tarmac,
a yardful of children, a tide, a flood
already moving away. I want to call her back,

I'm faint, suddenly starved with the lack
of her, and determined that she should
know, all sealed like a bomb in her anorak.

Grip the wheel. Radio on. The yakety-yak
of today's talking heads on How to Be Good.
The morning is moving away. I want to call her back.

This is what it's like to be left slack,
the cord frayed like I knew it would.
She is sealed like a bomb in her anorak,
already moved away, and I can't call her back.

I saw the sculpture 'My Daughter in Winter Costume' (1922) at the Boston Athenaeum Library in 2010, in the exhibition *John Storrs: Machine-Age Modernist*. This daughter had a stoutness that delightedly flouted modernism's lean, rawboned lines. This daughter was robust, and in that she seemed safe, even though she stood quite alone on a plinth in the centre of a large room.

Her endearing rotundity — the confusion of where she began and ended — led me to the villanelle. I admire this form because though it mandates nineteen lines the return of those repeated lines means you might, if so moved, outrun the nineteen lines and never come back. It makes sense that the form has its possible origins in dance: the *virelai*, a category of French *chanson* depending, like the *rondeau*, on the tight whirl of rhyme and reprise. (I might also suggest the villanelle's relationship to 'Lanigan's Ball', where line steps out and line steps in again.)

The poem was written before I met my stepdaughter, Niamh. But a poem can, I suppose, lie in wait for its return. I caught up with it, and it with me, one morning when zipping Niamh into a sleeveless quilted jacket. This jacket, deeply red and flocked with pink flowers, belonged to another child. Her name is written in forbidding felt tip pen inside the collar: Lily. That the jacket was so fat, and that it had looked after the child of a dear friend, seemed as heartening as that chubby sculptural form on the plinth in Boston.

That jacket was much-loved and is now outgrown. The villanelle form is perhaps a net: all those lines shuttling back and forth in repetition, still trying for the same thing as the poem — which is to say, safety.

SHEILA O'HAGAN

September the Fourth

At four a.m. today my lover died.
He didn't reach for me or call my name,
Dreaming he would waken by my side,
But turned his face and shuddered as some shame
Or haunting shook him and his mouth gave cry
To a portentous and unearthly pain.

Between darkness and dawn that cry of pain
And nothing warm has touched me since it died.
An ethos of cold starlight I can't name
Possessed my love while he lay by my side,
Something strange, unhuman, born of shame.
He said not goodbye, called out or cried.

Some ghost or spirit left his mouth that cried
Out and he'd gone from me, had gone in pain
Into an alien world, yet as he died
He drew my spirit to him, gave her my name.
Something possessed him as he left my side,
His face was turned away as though in shame.

I took his absent face and murmured shame
To that which claimed him, for my love had cried
As though some shady trafficking in pain,
Some curse or Judas kiss by which he died
Unknowingly in another's name,
Had come to term as he lay down beside

The one he loved. Perhaps lying by his side,
Fearful in sleep. I had called up that shame
And he, my love, unknowingly had cried

Out in redemption for another's pain,
As though a chosen victim. My love died
Because some cursed spirit took his name.

For he was loved and honoured in his name
And I, as I lay sleeping by his side
Guarding his innocence, knew of no shame.
On the strange cusp of dark and dawn he cried
Aloud so strange my heart burned loud with pain.
Not one warm thought has touched me since he died.

Still I call his name. All hope had died.
My unspent love's my pain. I have not cried.
Such is winter's shame, all's bare outside.

My own state or method of composing was quite different from Ted's (McNulty), my partner in life and in verse to whom the poem 'September the Fourth' is dedicated, a sort of rhapsody or, to put it more prosaically, a mood of excitement or discovery.

I suffered an addiction that might or might not end in a 'benediction'. The waste bin was almost entirely filled by me, I worked fast on an old Amstrad. Once a poem started to reveal itself I found the versatility of a computer very apt.

I didn't stay sacramentally still as Ted did in our apartment that had high windows that overlooked Stephen's Green. I moved around quietly, looking into books, notes, anything that might feed that unveiling. Ted was very satisfied by the physicality of writing,; when he used pencils they were plain and sharpened; his pen would be a favourite, heavy on his hand so he was aware of it.

His first draft would go down the left side of the margin; beside it on the right would be his corrections, his re-write.

Poems in progress were filed under *Ships in Dock*; poems sent out to publications were *Ships at Sea*.

It would be glib, but not far off the mark, to describe 'September the Fourth' as my *Ship at Sea* poem, homage to the man he was — it's an extant poem, a *caoin* that announced itself unexpectedly, surprising in its passion the 'shame' of that other name called out at the moment of death, the pull of old love (what Joyce enunciated so well in 'The Dead') — one of Ted and my own favourite stories.

A late bloomer, like Ted, what time we had together was lived in a 'fever', as it should have been. When I look back on it now, I will finish with Ted's poem 'The Last Suit'.

> In the men's department
> of Clerys, the pensioner
> shy of what he's doing
> asks for something dark.
> then feels satin lining
> around his shoulders,
> and the trousers like boards
> down his legs,
> and he will tell
> the fitter if he asks
> the suit is for a christening.

NESSA O'MAHONY

Lament for a Shy Man

He would have hated this,
the man who turned his face
to hedgerows rather than risk
a greeting on a country road.
It would be another death
to know the details
of his life were being discussed
over breakfast, at church gates,
in hazy snugs as far as
Moate and Mullingar.

In 1996, an elderly man called Tommy Casey was found beaten to death on the kitchen floor of his small cottage in Oranmore, Co. Galway. He had been assaulted and tied up during a burglary and left to die from his injuries. Details of the attack made front-page news for weeks. Newspaper articles all commented on the reclusive nature of the man, his extreme shyness, the habit of turning "his face to the ditch rather than greet passers by" as *The Irish Independent* would later put it.

Tommy Casey's lonely death was an outrage, but the wall-to-wall coverage, the minute focus on the life of a man who'd chosen to live behind a veil of secrecy, seemed at the time an even greater outrage. I kept thinking how appalled he'd be at the headlines, how mortified by the stories circulating about him.

His poem started out as something far longer, more journalistic; the original draft had around six or seven stanzas, I recall. But I found myself excising more and more detail, realizing that with all the biographical facts, I too was guilty of the sensationalism I sought to indict. So I cut back to its essence: the sense of privacy and shame such a man might have experienced. Of course, the final irony is that I could never know how Tommy Casey would have reacted. This poem arose from an attempt to imagine the world through his eyes; empathy has always been a starting point in my writing.

The older I get, the less sure I am about what constitutes success in poetry. Objectively, this poem garnered accolades (a national competition win, a Hennessey short-listing); subjectively it taught me about distillation, about honesty. I'm glad I wrote it.

MARY O'MALLEY

The Gulls at Fastnet

Condemned to endless flight
always attracted by the ship's light.

Inside I watch their eyes. A blink
makes each bird separate from the troupe
weary, wings bending the wind

in certain geometry which if decoded
might eradicate disease or at least
provide the mathematical basis for hope.

But who's interested in tired birds?
An hour ago, inches above the waves
a shoal of flying fish mimicked

them and all was silver and black-tipped
as houndstooth, lit so that those on the deck
might have been wearing 1940s frocks

Once, your lungs strove like this, each breath
Such labour you wanted it to stop, just finish

the scientists smoking,
the Frenchman taking a deckchair and leaning
towards his colleague with a light

in formal black, almost touching her bare shoulder,
leaning like they did then before everything
had to be spelled out. Instead they wear

hard hats and wet gear, monitors, with microscopes
everywhere. At least he is offering a light
and she is smoking. White dwarves

slo-mo across the screen. Outside a gannet dives
and creatures that want nothing to do with our affairs
veer and turn on their suspected gyres

old experts on wave dynamics.
The gulls, like silver shavings, fly on because they must
until dawn releases them, and us.

I chose this poem partly because of length. My first choice,
'Sea Road, No Map' is too long for inclusion, but had the
same occasion, a voyage on a marine research ship and
conversations with scientists.

This is a poem about surface, a ship travelling on the skin of
a sea several fathoms deep, passing over mountains and reefs,
gulfs and the occasional wreck, and the screws biting into the
waves for purchase.

A trip in the company of scientists lowering instruments
and measuring luminescence, tracking the paths of waves of
tiny creatures with their workmanlike implements and writing
down what they found.

The day on a ship is monastic, ordered and safe. Its limits are
clarifying, its freedom exhilarating. It is a life I would have liked
to live, one in which I have found comfort and rhythm, and
echoes of sea journeys from Homer to *The Book of Invasions*.

The vessel had a clean strong shape, afloat on a sea of
mutability. There was illusion of permanence and it is as close
to peace as I have ever come.

This is a poem from that shifting surface. I choose it for its
location and compromises with form and language. Perhaps I
also chose it to remind me of those moments of grace, what
Joseph Brodsky refers to as "moments of spotting the elements
of your own composition being free".

LEANNE O'SULLIVAN

The Station Mass

for Rita Seer

Everything scrubbed down and scrubbed again.
Every room followed its own lighted passage,
singing out its corners and the polished dark.
The makeshift altar set, she moved from room
to room, pelting the floors with her slippered walk.

Down in the kitchen the beautiful spread of meals,
the little locks and curls of butter flaring sunlight.
We were like her sentry guards in doorways,
barefoot, sweeping for motes and blemishes
or eyeing hiding places that suddenly stood clear.

Roses, silver, lace; the glasses breathed against.
Then the gravel-call of priests and neighbours
up the lane and we were all come and go again,
herself gone ahead of us down the last swept path,
snapping incantations, scattering light.

I wrote this poem during my one month stay at
Annaghmakerrig in 2010. I write very slowly, and I had
started this poem about a year and a half before it was
finished.

Altogether the poem filled one big foolscap book — which
is one reason this is a 'touchstone' poem, I felt that I had
apprenticed myself to this poem and the work it would take to
make it come true.

It had different incarnations, including a prose piece,

exploring how my Grandmother, Rita O' Sullivan (Seer), would prepare the house for the Stations. For better or worse, I loved watching the woman's work in the kitchen, before the priest, neighbours and Holy Ghost would descend on the house.

It was, for me, mystical, mysterious, golden: for a woman to prepare the way for another mystery. My Grandmother's work in the kitchen was always more interesting. There is nothing more awesome or wonder-filled than the narratives we imagine and the rituals we create to manifest them.

KARL PARKINSON

A Love Letter to Reinaldo Arenas

I love you Reinaldo,
you fantastic faggot, marvellous maricon,
picaro Prince of summer, yes I love you.

I loved you when you were a rabbit chased by hares.

I loved you when you were little Celestino
writing poems on trees in Oriente, and
your Grandpa tried to kill you with the hatchet.

I loved you when you were a butterfly caught in a net.

I loved you when you ran away to 'Che'
in the mountains, when you sweated cutting
Castro's ten million-tons of sugar cane down.

I loved you when you were the funk of sex in men's toilets.

I loved you when they jailed you with murderers,
because you were queer, where you wrote your novel
Farewell To The Sea and the guards they burned it,

so you wrote it again and had it smuggled out
up a drag queen's hole. Yes, this is why I love you
Reinaldo, you faggot, maricon, picaro, queer, sissy,

nancy, bumboy, cock-sucker, homo, Latin Proust,
beardless Whitman, peasant poet who loved the bodies
of two-thousand men, magical realist Jean Genet.

I loved you when you were mango juice spit in the air.

I loved you as you got the *San Lazaro* out of Cuba
to the shore of America, where you died uncared for,
because insurance, well, it costs mucho dollars, you see?

I loved you when you saw death playing with a bicycle wheel.

I loved you as you suicided in that small apartment,
I wish I was there holding your hand, stroking your face,
closing your eyelids, and kissing your forehead goodbye.

I listen to your voice in the waves of the sea, words bearing
with a panther's grace, and I fall on the sand with the taste
of your salt on my lips and yes, yes Reinaldo I love you.

L ike every poet, I have my themes that keep coming up; in
the collection I'm working on now, some of those themes
are: Death, the life of the writer, the role of the writer
in the world, spiritual and/or artistic power versus political/
religious power or economic/corporate power, artists who have
affected or influenced my life and art.

One night as I sat in bed, I began to think of Reinaldo
Arenas the great dissident Cuban writer, and all of these themes
that had/have been in my mind, coalesced upon the image of
Reinaldo and I sat up and took pen and notebook in hand and
thought what can I say to him? Can I write a letter to him and
send it to the land of the dead, and so the words came, flowing
like the river to the sea, a gift of a poem, and I guided it gently
on to the page for Reinaldo, to say well, yes all that happened,
all that suffering yet all that power in the words, to say yes I
poet, love you, poet, that is all I can give you, love, that is all I
can give the reader, love.

I knew when I'd finished that first draft that I had reached
some new maturity in my writing, that I had jumped across

a bridge and landed in a new place of power, gone deeper into my own heart's core and therefore deeper into the heart of humanity, and so this poem marks a spot on which I can stand and say "There, I leaped forward to Renaldo and found something more of me".

PAUL PERRY

In the Spring of My Forty-First Year

I was never young or always was —
and was forever on my way

to becoming someone
whom I could sit or be silent with

running through Marley Park
or up into Glencullen

with the rain on my face
my heart thirsting for nothing

no clock to keep time
no finish line either

the ease of distance in my legs
the breath bringing me

to whom I am
away from the country

across time
to where we are

and back again to rough terrain
where I am no one no where

a figure in the evening
passing

my footfall ringing silently
through Pearse's Park

or Pine Forest or farther still
wordless and weightless

moving like the sun-scattered light
at once and irrevocably

towards you

'In the Spring of My Forty-First Year' is a poem preoccupied
with time; time present, time past and time passing. It's
a poem interested in stillness and silence, a poem which
tries to slow the race of time down — not so much an argument
with the self, as Yeats would have it, but a quiet word with the
self, something which suggests an honest dialogue.

I have since writing the poem been reading Akhmatova's 'I
have taught myself to live quietly and wisely' on a daily basis,
almost as a form of prayer you could say. 'In the Spring ...' is a
journey towards finding the spiritual in poetry again, my own way
of teaching myself to live quietly and wisely. It revisits, by name,
many of the places I ran through while growing up — I mean run
as in play and also in the athletic sense, a sport which took up
much of my life as a youngster and school-boy and brought me to
America where I stayed for ten formative years in the 1990s.

Whereas before, many of my poems got carried away with
their own heady lyric, 'In the Spring ...' slows things down.
In my eyes, the poem is about realisation and acceptance.
Getting older does that, settling down, putting down roots
after a peripatetic and transient existence heretofore has been
important and with this poem whose trajectory is both forward
and back and in the moment, if that can be, I have tried to
articulate something of that movement.

In that sense it is a touchstone poem for me, one which
signals a new stage in my writing and life. I don't know if it
is my best poem, or will be my most anthologised poem —

perhaps some of my more politicised, rhapsodic poems may be more representative of the jaunty lyric I had created, an identity which was in constant flux, but the steady pulse in this poem, the meditative space of silence and acceptance which it aspires to seems to me to capture something of which sounds real and meaningful.

There's not much more I could ask of a poem.

BILLY RAMSELL

Complicated Pleasures

We were in bed together listening to Lyric,
to a special about the Russians,
when the tanks rolled into Babylon.

For a second I could feel their engines,
and the desert floor vibrating,
in the radio's bass rattling your bedroom
as the drums expanded at the centre of the Leningrad,
as those sinister cellos invaded the melody.

We'd been trying, for the hell of it,
to speak our own tongue
and I was banging on about Iberia when your eyelids closed:
'*Tá do lámh I mo lámh*' I whispered '*ar nós cathair bán*
sna sléibhte lárnach, d'anáil ar nós suantraí na mara i mBarcelona.
Codhladh sámh.'

But as I murmured 'sleep, my darling, sleep' into your sleeping ear
I found myself thinking of magnets
of what I'd learned in school about the attraction of opposites,
that the two of us, so similar,
could only ever repel one another.

For the closer I clutched your compact body
the further apart we grew.

You have eleven laughs
and seven scents
and I know them like a language.
But what will it matter when the bombs start falling
that you could never love me?

Then you turned in my arms
and it was midnight again on the beach at Ardmore,
when the starlight collected in some rock pool or rain pool
among the ragged crags at the water's edge
and the two of us sat there
and we didn't even breathe
determined not to the disturb that puddle's flux,
the tiny light-show in its rippling shallows,
the miniature star-charts that for a moment inhabited it.

And you whispered that the planets, like us, are slaves to
magnetism,
gravity's prisoners, as they dance the same circles again and
again,
and that even the stars ramble mathematically,
their glitter preordained to the last flash.

You turned again as I looked at the night sky
through your attic window
and thought of the satellites
gliding and swivelling in their infinite silence,
as they gaze down on humanity's fumbling,
on you and me, as you sniffled against my neck
and the drumming, drumming flooded your bedroom,
on powerful men in offices pressing buttons
that push buttons in powerful men,
on the tanks, like ants, advancing through the wilderness.

Those pitiless satellites, aware of every coming conflagration
and what would burn in it,
knowing for certain in their whispering circuits
that, like our island's fragile language,
like Gaudi's pinnacles and the *Leningrad* symphony,
— even worse — like your teeth and our four hands,
the very stars through which they wander would be gone,

those brittle constellations with the billion sinners that orbit them,
extinguished in a heartbeat, absolved instantly,
as if your hand had brushed the water slowly once.

St. Declan's Cathedral, Ardmore, County Waterford, 12th Century

Think of the hands that rendered them: these carved ovals, this series of blunt ciphers, these spiralling concave hieroglyphs. Some are smudged and smoothed past all decipherability, mere stubs of pictures now. And two, alas, at either end are robbed or hollowed out completely, their arcana missed and missing. But there's still the singing recognisability of Solomon, evaluating mothers in his throne room, of Adam petrified with want before the pomegranate tree.

Think of their careful maker etching there, bloody-knuckled in February, while the tide comes in and goes out again on this South-Eastern Irish coastline. Think of him drilling and divoting into fierce then suddenly flaking sandstone strata.

It will take him all winter and spring, this arcade of thirteen images, these reminders carved into the once and wannabe cathedral, into the roofless nave's west gable: the thresher still with his flail aloft, the charioted knight's baptism.

It's time itself that his chisel's cutting into; not only the nine or so centuries between him and us, that his efforts will endure, will resist at least for the greater part, but also the vastness separating his brute tools and the happenings they remember. Think of the leagues and millennia between Jerusalem and Munster, between the iron-age and this Irish journeyman, between this damp pastoral and the blood-stained fidelities of the desert.

He leans almost sideways on his bockety scaffold. Absorbed, he forgets his chapped hands. In Louviers, Richard Lionheart is settling, at least temporarily, his differences with the French.

The English language is still only a rumour in these parishes. He strikes and sandstone splashes down. The Georgians have shattered the Ildenizids at Shamkor. The tide comes in and goes out again. He measures, chisels, measures. In Constantinople, Alexius III, cautious, vicious, fair-skinned beyond reckoning, adjusts to the throne and the machinery of government.

Slievemore Deserted Village

Curlew calls over the lake
as the rain clears.
Brittle wisps hiss, like
phone wires to an island.
Low cloud communicates
with famine ridges.

And in the ruins, I imagine
thin limbs of victims
outstretched to bridge the time.
In shame I retreat alone.
Their grandparents ageing gracefully now
in Pennsylvania and Chicago.

Diminished grass is slowly consumed.
Rushes enjoy a sinister revenge.
Their creeping paralysis ruthless
even in the most sacred places.
In the distance a figure approaches,
stumbles across the bog onto a track.

He disappears now and then in the hollows.
Smoked like a Moroccan street trader
he offers me a load of breast turf,
as if the boatloads of grain wouldn't leave the quay,
as if magpies wouldn't pick our eyes out,
as if grass wouldn't melt in our mouths.

I grew up singing 'Tantum Ergo' in the school choir and listening to Jimi Hendrix, driving cattle to a fair and learning about the Punic wars, watching the Virginian on a Saturday night and playing handball with tinkers in the village alley.

There was always contradiction, absurdity, the common brutality and the elemental always playing its adult games in the unfenced garden of my childhood. Hailstones and whitethorn blossoms, sin and the Jesuit missions, drunk bachelors and gentile ladies, wild mountainy men who drank warm blood in the slaughter house, cold men who waited a generation to inherit land and always the dead trying to claw through the gossamer curtain.

Weather and seasons can't be ignored living on the edge of an ocean as we danced to whatever tune it fired at us, while times' callous ratcheting clinked to punctuate the melancholic silences.

I captured a stray donkey on the bog road tackled him and stumbled after Patrick Kavanagh's ghost along the drills of Kerr's Pinks. I looked up at reeks of hay in October coloured weather and cut the horns of mad cows we bought in Connemara. I travelled to Kyrgyzstan and photographed a sheep fair only to be photographed in Maam Cross with my own sheep a month later.

All this leaks into the poetry together with the ordinary losses and triumphs of a father and public servant working for Mayo County Council. No single poem is representative of my work but I venture 'Slievemore Deserted Village' as it contains west of Ireland themes and the shadow of history which leaks into the present, constantly.

MAURICE RIORDAN

Badb

I was walking where the woods begin
with an almost sheer drop to the river
— so that I was eye level with the tops
of nearby trees and higher than the branch
when I came upon the crow sitting there,
so close I could have touched her with a stick.
She was creaturely and unwary, as the wind
bore her away and brought her back.
We shared the same tangy woodland smells,
the same malt-pale October sunlight.
Then I must have made a sound,
for she came alert and looked at me.
And, in that interval before the legs
could lift her weight from the branch,
as the beak sprang open to deliver
its single rough vowel, she held me off
with a look, with a sudden realignment
of the eyes above the gorping mouth.
It is the look known to legend and folk belief
— though also an attribute useful for a bird
without talons or guile to defend it.
Then she was gone, in a few wing beats
indistinguishable from her fellows wheeling
above the trees, carrying on their business,
neighbourly and otherworldly.

It surprises me that I often forget the genesis of a poem and how it gets written. There are exceptions. One of these is 'Badb', which was written in 1995. Christopher Reid, then poetry editor at Faber, asked for contributions to a small anthology to mark Ted Hughes's sixty-fifth birthday. I very much wanted to come up with a poem. But it seemed a hopeless wish. Then I remembered an 'encounter' I had as a solitary adolescent with a crow, when I found myself — as described in the poem — very close to one. So I set out to describe that incident. It took some time. A friend told me my 'finished' draft was twice too long. It became a race against the clock to cut it down to size. Yet the process of doing so was a lesson in how economising the detail of a poem can release its spirit. Somewhere along the route I gave it the title 'Badb'. She is the Old Irish goddess of the battlefield — suitably obscure, I felt, not to sound too portentous. I wanted an effect both magical and matter-of-fact to honour equally Hughes's interest myth and his descriptions of creatures. One particular detail I was pleased with was the adjective 'gorping'. It's a dialect word used by D.H. Lawrence in his poem 'Fish'. I felt pretty sure Hughes would approve of my theft. But when the poem was printed in *A Parcel of Poems* (the booklet that was his birthday gift), an editor or proofreader had changed 'gorping' to 'gawping'. Alas, Hughes was never to read the poem in its corrected form.

Firelight

I'd light the fire without meaning to,
I'd light it without noticing,
kindling and coal using my hands
to combust on the very warmest of days.

You in the light green chair, me
in the dark green, we'd sit, fire
flowering between us, its black nightgowns
slipping to the floor. Already

memorable, the coal we burn
re-deposited within us,
mine of ripeness, seam of grace.
Where unknown others sat before

and unknown others will again
we'd take our time. Fire privy
to our intimacies, fire privy
to the unspoken questions:

What is the price of seclusion?
What have we missed, being childless?
Its mild blast on our skin always
a reminder, a hint of a darkness

burnt into human skin in suburbs far
from an explosion. Mask of Hiroshima,
shadow scorched into all our flesh.
Good servant, bad master, fire insists.

Last thing we'd lie awake and watch
dying flames infiltrate the bedroom

and dapple the walls. We'd hear
the soft toc as clinker hit the pan.

A sudden flare might send me stumbling
to check all was well. I'd hurry back,
sobered, in violation
of a privacy. To see the fire gently

collapsing, talking to itself, heating
empty chairs, was to know what
the world would look like when
we're not there. Was to be thin air.

'Firelight' was the first poem I'd written which I felt some
slight confidence in. It's a poem I still often use to start a
reading, because I think it sets a particular tone. I think
it was the first poem I wrote where I felt I had gone beyond the
personal, where my own voice might have surrendered just a bit
to some deeper voice.

I have always loved coal fires. Sitting by the hearth is of
course the most clichéd of images of domestic bliss, but I've
always been fascinated by the fact that the fire you sit so close
to has the immediate power to consume all you think of as
yourself. So, where you feel most at home is where you are
closest to cosmic homelessness; where you feel most settled is
also most unsettling.

That sense of insecurity at the heart of security is one I find
I keep returning to in poems: it has contributed to the titles of
each of my collections so far. And as well as insecurity, there is
the sense of continuity. To the Greeks and Romans, the fire was
where the dead maintained a presence among the living. The
fire was where two realms interpenetrated. I like the sense of
absence, of ghostliness and mystery inside the fact of presence.

I liked the form of the poem too. The stanzas seemed solid, though many run on into the next one: this seemed to fit the content of the poem. There are of course bits of it I feel are crude and undeserved, particularly the sixth stanza. But I felt the last three stanzas worked better than anything I had written up to then. The word 'toc' seems to me exact. The rhyme of 'there' and 'air' in the last line catches the theme of the poem.

GABRIEL ROSENSTOCK

Ophelia an Phiarsaigh

*'We knew her well, and she was the most nobly planned of all the
women we have known.'* — An Piarsach

Bhí an fhoirmle ag an Athair Tom
an chantaireacht
na briathra is na frásaí
an tslí cheart chun iad a rá
is aige a bhí an phaidir
an rithim agus an tuinairde chuige
pé rud a thabharfá air
ortha is dócha
nó an mantra a bhí ann?
bhí ar a chumas an t-anam
a ghlaoch ar ais
ar ais i gcolainn Eibhlín
Ophelia an Phiarsaigh
Eibhlín chaomh Nic Niocaill
mo chreach, Eibhlín bhocht
a bádh is í ar cuairt ar an mBlascaod
ní fhéadfadh sé é a dhéanamh
ní dhéanfadh
ní thiocfadh na focail chuige
níor thánadar
ní thiocfaidís óna bhéal
ó bhíodar aige ambaist
an tAthair Tom — Asarlaí —
na siollaí suairce sin a mheallfadh anam
Eibhlín Nic Niocaill
an spiorad íonghlan aici á chuimilt ar ais ina corp goirt
le cogarnaíl ársa
bhí fhios ag cách é
bhí fhios ag an domhan mór go rabhadar aige

239

ach is faoi ghlas istigh ann a bhíodar

ní balbh a bhí na mná caointe:
            mo ghraidhn thú, a Eibhlín,
       mo ghraidhn do mháthair,
mo ghraidhn go brách í!

abair liom an fhoirmle
atá in ann cor a chur sa stair!
thug an tAthair Tom chun na huaighe leis é mar rún

Pearse's Ophelia

'We knew her well, and she was the most nobly planned of all the
women we have known.'
— P. H. Pearse

Father Tom had the formula
the chant
the words and phrases
the exact way to utter them
he had the prayer
the rhythm and pitch of it
the tone
whatever it was
the charm
incantation
was it a mantra
he could have called the soul
calling it back
back into the body of Eibhlín
Pearse's Ophelia
Eibhlín Nic Niocaill
alas, poor Eibhlín
drowned on a visit to the Blaskets

he couldn't do it
wouldn't do it
couldn't say the words
they wouldn't come to him
wouldn't come out of his mouth
oh he had them alright
Father Tom — Conjuror —
every precious syllable to snare the soul
of Eibhlín Nic Niocaill
massaging the pure spirit back into her briny body
with ancient whisperings
everyone knew it
everyone knew he had them
but they were locked inside him
frozen

keening women found words to wail her:
                mo ghraidhn thú, a Eibhlín,
        mo ghraidhn do mháthair,
mo ghraidhn go brách í!

What is the formula
that can change history?
Father Tom brought his cold secret with him to the grave.

Translated by the author

W ho during the 1916 centenary celebrations has been left out of the picture? I thought of Eibhlín Nic Niocaill or Eveleen Constance Nicolls (1884-1909) who didn't live long enough to witness the Easter Rising, or take part in it: had she married Pearse, might things have been in any way different?

Who was she? She had a First Class Honours Degree in Modern Literature and spent some time in France and Germany. She worked for a while in the Paris branch of the Gaelic League. How many of our arts graduates today would think of doing such volunteer work for the sake of the language?

James H. Cousins (another fascinating figure of that era) writes: "At a gathering of girl friends before Eveleen's departure on her Kerry holiday the question had been asked as to the kind of death they would desire. Eveleen had answered, 'To be drowned saving another!'" And that's exactly what happened. There was some speculation that she may have been secretly engaged to P. H. Pearse. Would history have changed in any way if Fr. Tom Jones (yet another remarkable figure) had managed to revive her?

In what way does the poem express my vision of life or my vision of poetry? I have always liked mixing the esoteric with the exoteric, the old and the new, the strange with the familiar. One of the tasks of the poet is to be a guardian of the portals to mystery and memory. The subject matter of this poem and its mantric echoes may not have significance for all readers but it's a poem that reaffirms my conviction that life is charged with multiple mysteries. (Cousins, by the way, would end up in India and have an influence on the poetics of Sri Aurobindo, but that's another story).

Do the attempts to revive Eibhlín mirror our failed attempts to revive the language? I wasn't conscious of that when writing the poem. I don't think one needs to be conscious of all the strands that are woven into a poem.

Sunday Miscellany (RTÉ Radio 1) asked me had I a poem with a 1916 flavour. I hadn't (though I had many Irish translations of poems associated with the era). Had I not been asked, the poem would have been unborn. And that's another mystery, isn't it?

COLM SCULLY

What news, Centurions?

'What news, Centurions, what news of Cork?'

Only the mossed green pavements and the tired slabs,
the gullies wandering into iron grates
whose imprints solemnly betray their age,
cast in Bristol or in Harrogate.

Only the uncouth houses on the narrow streets,
the shambled skylines with a hint of grey,
the topsy turvy roofs and gable ends
crawling up hills in ever varying lines.

Even the new and clean edifice confounds the eye,
the glass constructs in blue metal frames.
Tarpaulin green coppered domes and plates
vie with exotic timbers in panelled walls.

None of them know their place amid the red and white
sand and limestone structures of the past.
Aspiring towers cast long shadows in the river,
elysian dreams, well short of Elysium.

'What of its people, what news of them?'

As you left them consul, except they've changed,
swollen in numbers since your last campaign.
Now every tongue on earth can be heard.
Close your eyes on Marlboro Street and listen.

'I hear them, the tongues mixing,
the brittle patter of Pana with the foreign threads.

I know their songs so well and ask —
Are they as happy with their new found wealth,
their ivory towers, their elegant lanes?'

They are still a rough and tumble people,
children of country folk a generation gone.
Crude laughter still falls hard from open windows.
Sarcasm envelopes their muddled talk.

They still walk with the unsure gait of deprivation,
though decades have fallen since it held them in its grasp.
Their sad eyes and rough ruddy faces
speak more of past news than of the now.

They celebrate as well as ever.
When their teams win, crowds gather in Daunt Square.
They sing and drink high praise into the early hours,
then leave the forlorn, rain wet dingy streets

strewn with detritus.

My poems are often triggered by an over-heard phrase which leads on to a first line. That was what happened with the title poem of my collection *What News, Centurions?* While working as an engineer in a vast portacabin in Kinsale on a freezing cold winter morning, I overheard the only other person in the office hail the arrival of some colleagues from Cork with the salutation, "What news, Centurions, what news of Cork?" While reflecting on it later I decided I had to reply to the question.

It was a great vehicle for me to investigate my thoughts on Cork City and its people, something that is indelibly linked with my identity. I grew up and have spent nearly all my life here. My father was born in a house on Patrick Street in 1929,

244

you can't get much more Cork than that.

I do not try to paint Cork in a romanticised light of crubeens and Shandon, rather I aim to investigate the often incongruous nature of love for a place which is not one of architectural note. Sometimes I am surprised by how a poem builds its own unintended circularity, as with this case where I start with the old paving slabs, rise to the pinnacle of the Elysian, and finally end once more in the gutters strewn with detritus.

The poem represents my development as a poet because it somehow brought together a number of the techniques and themes I prefer — dialogue, fantastical situations (the locus of the poem is an impossibility: a Roman Consul seeking news from his centurions of contemporary Cork), my city and its people, historical conceits, sense of identity. The distance of two thousand years aids objectivity — it is my attempt at removing sentiment from a relationship loaded with it.

JOHN W. SEXTON

Sixfaces and the Woman of Nothing

Sixfaces is asleep in the grass, all of his eyes
closed at once. He has been asleep for so long
that the grasses have begun to take root in his mind.
Two lovers enter one of his mouths and begin to couple
on his tongue. Bats have entered at his twelve ears,
their excrement layered night after night.
Sixfaces is dreaming six times over, six different dreams.
His six-sided brain is throbbing with thought,
but he'll remember not one single thing.

A woman of nothing finds him lying asleep.
She has never seen anything so curious before,
a wheel of six faces. She would lift it but she has no hands,
gently toe it over the grass but she has no feet. She'd kiss
the six mouths one by one but she has no mouth of her own.
House martins emerge from his twelve nostrils,
catch insects in flight and then return. Bees
have built their hives in the ducts at the corners of his eyes.

How beautiful he is, fast asleep. Wild pigs emerge
from one of his mouths, go rooting amongst the trees.
Monkeys scramble up the lines of his foreheads,
disappear into his thick hair. *Wake up, wake up,*
thinks the woman of nothing, but her thoughts are soundless.
She lies down beside him, begins to doze. Soon she is asleep,
her nothing head dreaming of nothing. She becomes the space
that he'll see if he wakes.

It seems to me that there are times when a poem should hide its process and the poet's motive. Indeed, sometimes these things should only exist in the poem like leukocytes within its bloodstream: aiding the body and its functions, but utterly invisible. What preoccupies us as individuals is oftentimes best expressed in our poetry slantways.

A major preoccupation of mine that enters the poetry more times slant than explicitly is the situation of my twenty-nine-year-old son, Matthew. Matthew is autistic and has the comprehension of a young child; he has very little expressive language, and struggles to both understand and be understood.

However, he does have gifts, amongst them a talent for drawing and painting: another gift appears to be the comprehension of invisible beings, which he refers to as angels. The nature of his congress with these angels, however, is unquantifiable, because he cannot express it to us in any expansive way, lacking language as he does. But, notwithstanding his gifts and struggles, what he imbues in the life around him, beyond any doubt, is a palpable Grace.

One day I was rereading Hesiod's *The Theogony* when I became cognisant of an obvious parallel. The description of the Titans, including the three Cyclopes and the three Hecatonchires, suddenly struck me as being not so much of creatures with immense or near-angelic bearing, but of creatures with physical or mental handicap. And it was in this moment that I had an epiphany; and thus suddenly my way into a poem of a very personal nature.

The Theogony tells us that the Muses came to Hesiod while he was tending his sheep on Mount Helicon; they endowed upon him the insight of poetry. In a sense, I suppose, Hesiod's insight came upon me by transference on that day when I received a way into this poem of my own.

My Father, Long Dead

My father, long dead,
has become air

Become scent
of pipe smoke, of turf smoke, of resin

Become light
and shade on the river

Become foxglove,
buttercup, tree bark

Become corncrake
lost from the meadow

Become silence,
places of calm

Become badger at dusk,
deer in the thicket

Become grass
on the road to the castle

Become mist
on the turret

Become dark-haired hero in a story
written by a dark-haired child.

I like to think that every individual poem has an address: a dot on an imaginary map that we can point to definitively and say, right there, little poem, that's where you got your start. In thinking about creativity, I am drawn to Hartnett's quip '... like all poets I can foretell the past'.

The act of writing is not only a method of expression but a means of discovery. We can tell where a poem begins but can't always tell where it will end. The most satisfying writing for me is when a poem leads me to someplace unexpected.

This poem sprung from a conversation I had with three dead people. It was Christmas week and I was admonishing my mother and my mother-in-law for having died during Christmas six years previously. I was pointing out how their ill-timed departures had not only ruined that Christmas but had ruined every subsequent Christmas.

My father said nothing much, as was his habit, but looked rather pleased at having died years before them in June, with no great fuss. When the title of the poem came to me, 'My Father, Long Dead', I thought that the poem was going to be a blackly-humorous piece on the impossibility of forever ruining June.

The poem had its own ideas about what it wanted to say. Image after image manifested in celebration of a landscape; in celebration of my father, the first storyteller I knew. The poem became for me an affirmation of the creative impulse. It answered the question I didn't know I had asked.

It showed me the distinction between being from a place and being of a place. The storyteller entered the myth, became part of the story. As if the landscape, the story, the child, the father, the poem itself had already existed and I had just happened across them.

PETER SIRR

After a Day in the History of the City

What vagabond bones
and you, too, Ivar the Boneless,
come together now
stench of what plagues
thriving again
and everywhere one turns
places of execution

Who should not prefer
to cross the river
and walk in procession
down the aisle of his own cathedral
with Samuel
Metropolitan of Oxmantown
wanting nothing from him but his title

or say, with Peter Lewis, cathedral proctor
Today came with his men Tady the hellier
to renew the slates
after the heavy snows of Christmas and the frost

I've always been a bit obsessed by cities: the city I was born
in, those that I lived in when I left Ireland in my twenties,
the one that I live in now. Everything about cities interests
me. The architecture, the people and the social spaces where
they encounter each other, the history. The layers — that sense
you have in a city of dense occupation going back centuries.
It's hard to write about in some ways because a city is made up
of so many discrete experiences, and you're fooling yourself if
you think you can capture everything. In another, more recent

poem, I imagined being a mapmaker, who, having pinned down the buildings and streets, now wants to get to the real heart of things 'Now I want everything else. / I want to be a historian of footsteps,/a cartographer of hemlines and eyelids, / I want to catch what the pavements say // when they sing to each other.'

All this struck me more when I moved from the suburbs into the city centre, just opposite Christchurch Cathedral. To walk around the area was to feel the breath of the past on your shoulder, and I began to take an active interest in the history of the city. Which is how I ended up reading the accounts of the cathedral proctor, or accountant, Peter Lewis, for the year 1564–1565. This might seem like dry reading but I feasted on its meticulous detail: how much spent on ale, how much on slates, who the workmen were and what they were paid. This gets into the poem, as do elements of the earlier history. I wanted a sense of crowdedness, of mess, plague but also the sense of the city about its ordinary business of building and renewal. And I wanted to do that without writing a history lesson, with as little fuss as I could manage and ending with Lewis's own words, which are the lines I like most.

GERARD SMYTH

Taken

for Thomas Kinsella

First the city planners took away the old street
along with neighbours who had seen the changes.
They took away the barbershop, sweetshop, the grocery
on the corner that mainly sold bread and milk,
butter from a marble slab
and through the colder months bundled sticks
that burned to ash in the fires of New Row.
They took away the abattoir and back-lane stables,
the clothes lines and window ledges
holding pots of geraniums, the shoe factory
and the shortcut to the block of flats
named after an Easter patriot.

They took away all clues of history and tradition:
the hiding places and escape routes the Rebel
Irish used, the sites of execution,
the enclave of refuge for Huguenots persecuted
in the name of God. They disturbed the dust
that lay on the handiwork of ancient guilds,
pulled up foundations buried since
the first strangers put a name on what they saw.
They took away the cradle school
that was half for girls and half for boys,
and left no trace of the picture house
where the patrons paid half-price
to see Jim Hawkins sail in search of *Treasure Island*.

The discovery of a book of photographs of the streetscapes of my Dublin childhood and youth was, to an extent, responsible for awakening memories that led to the poem 'Taken'. The images in *The Past has a Great Future: Mick Brown's Dublin* were my touchstones of recollection, reminding me of that bygone city — a place, it has to be said, of some shabbiness and decrepitude yet dear to me — but Brown's evocative archive also reminded me of what was lost or, as the poem implies, "taken" from us during a chapter in the city's history when, it seemed to me, the blueprints of reconstruction showed little concern for history or heritage.

'Taken' is a Dublin poem but also a poem of protest written long after the events and circumstance to which it refers. Those events, well documented elsewhere, were the uprooting and removal of inner city communities, the bulldozing and destruction of long-standing streetscapes and, as a consequence, local traditions in the area in which I was born and grew up: The Liberties.

The cause of all this was the rush to replace the old with the new, the official obsession with road-widening to facilitate the burgeoning commuter traffic in from and out to the suburbs. Streets of character were ruinously replaced by four-lane highways that cut through the heartland (I am thinking in particular of High Street, Patrick Street and Clanbrassil Street).

This was the 1970s when it seemed that nothing was sacred: the refusal to preserve the site of the ancient Viking settlement on Wood Quay was the most appalling and infamous example of the policy-making that changed the fabric of an area that is the birthplace of the our capital.

In another poem called 'In the Brazen Head' I refer to that specific location as one of Dublin's "sites of desecration". In this poem, the site — unnamed — is where the city planners

pulled up foundations buried since
the first strangers put a name on what they saw.

I realise but make no apology for the fact that this poem has its notes of yearning for what probably had to change, but the changes and reconstructions could have been more sensitive to and preserving of "history and tradition", as well as "the dust that lay on the handiwork of ancient guilds".

MATTHEW SWEENEY

I Don't Want to Get Old

Let me make this clear, I don't want to
get old. I have no desire for loose, wrinkled
skin, or that redness in the face and nose
I see in the couple at the next table,
about to fly off for a week in Jamaica.
I understand, at last, my father's feelings
in his last months, though I don't share yet
his keenness to lie in the grave and sleep
forever. So long in one place sounds terrifying.
What about the music he gave his life to?
I don't imagine it's heard much down there.
And as for the illness that took my mother
away to another world (where the afternoon
before she died, she gave me and the long-
dead Johnny equal time, and didn't know
my sister) I'll pass on that, but I confess
I don't see much to relish in the alternative.
Already my legs are beginning to allow in
peculiar pains, and my hearing admits me to
surrealism. My eyesight, however, is sharp,
plus my hair is the colour it was when I
was that boy who lived on the golf-course,
who played so late he was accused of being
a nocturnal walloper. Is there any chance
at all of becoming that lithe fellow again?

I n my writing I have always tended to eschew the
autobiographical route that so many poets decide to take.
I've found it much more to my taste to imagine myself into
other people's heads. Any of the early poems I tried to write

in a purely autobiographical way seemed to me later to lack something, a trick of some kind that the imagination might have provided, so I took to avoiding such an approach.

This had its drawbacks, however. An interviewer once spent an hour quizzing me on why I was not autobiographical. She seemed very puzzled, even annoyed. The interview was not going well. In desperation I thrust my book at her and asked her to read a poem called 'Tube Ride to Martha's', where I'd stepped into the conscientious of the one unidentified casualty of the King's Cross underground fire, trying to imagine his last hours. To my surprise, and relief, she suddenly seemed to understand what I was trying to do.

It has often been the same, a resistance in readers to this oblique approach Why not say what happened, as the late Lowell poem puts it. But I didn't, and took to suggesting to friends and family who were trying to dig out autobiographical material in my poems that when I employed the first person pronoun it was safe to assume that I was employing a persona. This situation continued happily until I came to the collection *Horse Music,* which came out in 2013. Oh, there are enough weird and oblique poems in that (the title poems concerns horses talking Irish on an Aran island), but I had also to deal with elegies for my father, mother, and my younger sister, Blaithin. That brought the autobiographical rudely into the poems, like it or not — and however much I sometimes tried to hide it.

Then I embarked on a sequence of poems that was eventually published in a pamphlet by the Poetry Business in 2014, under the title *Twentyone Men and a Ghost.* This sequence took me by surprise and I realised fairly quickly I was writing about mortality, rather than masculinity. All the men I'd ever met and all the women too, came into it — and all of those had made me what I was. So I knew these Men poems constituted a kind of alternative autobiography.

There was also a kind of coming to terms with getting old in some of those poems, and this preoccupation continued in quite a few of the pieces I was writing for the collection I was then finishing. So when I was brought to Yorkshire to read for a festival from the Men pamphlet, and found myself having lunch in the hotel I was staying in, which unknown to me was the favoured place for all the very old, well-off locals to convene for lunch on that day, I was provoked — no, frogmarched — to write the poem I append with this. Writing it was a bit of a battle, however — all my resistance to autobiography objected strongly, and tried to derail the poem.

I found myself thinking of American poets I liked who tended to stick to the autobiographical approach — Lowell, Sharon Olds, Philip Levine. Bishop even — although there is a supreme detachment there. And I thought of a song I love by the unique singer-songwriter Tom Waits, 'I Don't Wanna Grow Up' (there's a wonderful video online showing Tom dressed up in some kind of superhero suit, careering round and round a yard on a diminutive child's tricycle, howling out the song).

Anyway, with all this support the poem got written, and it surprised me — so much that I begged my publisher to add it to the collection at a late stage. I'd come to feel that the focus on getting old, or not getting old, fitted the book very well. Also, all my most personal autobiographical stuff had come in — my father and mother, shortly before their deaths, my slowly failing health (or hypochondria), and the memory of (and indeed the wish to be again) the lithe golfer I was when I was fifteen. Heavy, naked stuff! Despite this though, don't expect to find only poems like this in the new book. There's plenty of weirdness there too.

And And And

In Chad a skinny woman treks half the day,
    two twenty-gallon petrol cans
nailed to a bamboo pole slung across her shoulders.
These she fills with brown water from a distant pool.
What song does she sing as she walks?

Our rivers swirl in December to the tops of their medieval bridges,
    and water birds come to drink
        in places they've not been seen before.
Are Ireland's floods the dust storms of Africa?

In my own native land a man smoking a 12-inch cigar,
    with jowls like a boar's head on a platter,
smirks with pleasure and scorn and warns his audience
        of the 'global warming hoax'
    invented by 'bed-wetting liberals'.

I know I live in a world where
    in the name of my nationality
billions of dollars go to support
strong-legged men with beards and skullcaps and Uzis —
        faces burned by the sun,
the tassels of prayer shawls sticking out
        from under their flak jackets,
men who speak in the accents of Brooklyn and Ukraine.

With their chainsaws and machetes
    they hack at the roots of ancient olive trees
        and make bonfires from that fragrant wood.
The lights of their condos shine from every hilltop.

These men, and their wives with babies on their hips,
    travel in armoured SUVs over highways off-limits
        to the native population
whose ancestors, twelve hundred years ago and more,
    built stone mansions in Jaffa and Jerusalem
        with fountains in their gardens
where jasmine and bougainvillea flowered and figs ripened,

whose geometricians floated a golden
        dome over the Al-Aqsa Mosque
    when Europe was mud and thatch and round arches,
vassals and illiterate barons and monks who spoke bad Latin.
Half-a-millennium ago they saw the shaggy-haired
    crusaders come to reconsecrate their holy shrines
        and then go back to where they came from.

    My country too was once the promised land
for settlers who arrived from another continent
    and set to work clearing the land and herding
        the inhabitants into reservations.

Yet I was among those who, when we were young,
    danced the Hora, sang 'Tzena, Tzena, Tzena'
and thought that 'a land without a people
    for a people without a land' was a swell idea.
In those days we little knew that a land without people
    would be secured by clearing the natives off
        their grazing lands, and out of their villages,
herding them into refugee camps and building a wall
    five hundred miles long
        to keep them out of the promised land.

In Gaza City 7,000 people crowd into one square kilometre,
    as compared to perhaps sixteen of us
        here on the slopes of Sliabh na mBan,

not counting the foxes and pheasants, dogs and cats,
sheep and cattle, wrens and crows, thrushes and robins,
and the grey wagtails
that come to our yard to drink, mistaking it for a stream.

What is someone who loves clocks and Georgian architecture,
William Morris wallpaper and old silver,
who would rather listen to Bach's B Minor Mass
than surf savethechildren.org,
would rather read John Ruskin's *Stones of Venice*
than Naomi Klein's column in *The Nation* —
What is someone like me
doing awake at this hour of the night?

Yet here I am cold in this chair, listening to the clock tick,
rendered sleepless by things
I know are badly wrong
but over which I have no control.
And I haven't even mentioned
the shaved-head men in hoodies
on the bridges of Dublin and London and New York,
nodding over a paper cup with pennies in it.
And the CEO of Goldman Sachs who makes $100 a minute
even when he's asleep,
while 85 per cent of the world's population survives
on less than 5¢ a day.
And I'm leaving out Columbine and Virginia Tech
and Fort Hood
and the 4.4 firearms for every household in the US.

And and and.

What's one voice against the corporations?
Against drillers for oil in the Alaskan wilderness,
slash-and-burn crews on the Amazon,

against the NRA and OPEC and AIPAC and Wall Street?
They know what they want, and to them
          democracy is no more than an inconvenience.
All I have is a pen,
          and life is getting shorter.
The world I have lived in is disintegrating bit by bit,
          crumbling into time like the ice caps at the poles.

I have chosen 'And And And' for inclusion. It seems appropriate to include a poem that addresses some of the pressing political issues of our own day: Israeli domination of a subject Palestinian population, the American culture of firearms, and income inequality under global capitalism.

Except for the proliferation of firearms in America, each of these issues affects Ireland as well as the rest of the world. Israeli colonialism, backed by American dollars, is a 21st century version of the British colonialism the 1916 martyrs threw themselves up against.

I wrote the poem as an American living in Ireland during one of its rainiest winters. The floodwaters of the Suir surged to the tops of the stone bridges that span it. So much water ran through our yard in Tipperary that pied wagtails, a river bird, came to drink form the freshets formed by the rains. Knowing that climate change is characterized by extremes — drought in one part of the world, excessive rainfall in others — I ask the question, "Are Ireland's floods the dust storms of Africa?"

'And And And' tries to speak to those places where the little world of one's personal life, one's love of things like 'clocks and Georgian architecture, / William Morris wallpaper and old silver,' the choral music of Bach, the writings of John Ruskin, comes up against the larger, disturbing world filled with poverty, homelessness, the obscene disparities between the haves and the have-nots: 'And and and,' in the words of the poem.

While I worry that the poem editorializes too much and

lacks the condensed, crafted quality I try to achieve in other poems, it is important to me as a wordsmith to address the larger, sometimes frighteningly ominous macrocosm that swirls around us.

JESSICA TRAYNOR

Scenes From a Poor Town

Street lights turn the black world orange,
the moon is a lie the canal repeats
and repeats.

A man on the bridge agrees;
see his shape blacken the moon on water
until it vanishes.

⤵

Outside the derelict convent a shape moves,
white-bibbed, sharp-beaked, the street lamp
caught in its eye.

⤵

On the North Strand bombs sleep
under floorboards, below the tideline,
nestled truffles.

Their intricacies perennial,
they glide through the night on greased rails;
the dark hours, the slow hours.

It's late October 2011, and I've come back from Edinburgh for a conference at the Open University in Belfast. My husband and I have recently packed in our jobs, in the depths of the recession, to move country. Our home in north inner city Dublin is rented to strangers, and we're living in a damp tenement flat in Dalry, surviving on tinned chickpeas from Lidl.

In the brightly lit Belfast conference room, there are free sandwiches and tea, and poets and academics talking about their practice. And while I'm listening to them with interest, that meandering part of my mind, the part that's loosely tethered, has drifted off to Ballybough and the North Strand. The vista of East Wall as seen from the North Strand Canal Bridge confronts me; sprawling, industrial, bereft, a tangle of glinting train tracks. And I think about a house my husband and I almost bought there before we settled in Ballybough; a semi-derelict property that we fondly christened 'the murder house'. It felt inside as if it was being reclaimed by the tidal silt, that it might sink into the ground at any moment. It transpired later that the new owners had the pleasant surprise of finding a cache of War of Independence-era guns beneath the floorboards, along with homemade bombs. I picture their shapes emerging, salt-encrusted, from a damp hole in the ground.

And then my mind drifts towards Summerhill, onto Rutland Street, and then to the convent on Portland Row, past the blank eyes of its windows. A penguin, stolen from Dublin zoo, had recently been found wandering there like some grotesque parody of the nuns that would have inhabited the convent.

And the final image is a memory of a man, standing alone, hood up, on the Ballybough Canal Bridge, staring into the water below. I hadn't seen his face. The night is clear and cold, and I conflate the memory with a news report of a young man drowning in that part of the canal on a winter's night, in the shadow of Croke Park. I never found his name in the news reports.

In the conference room, I write these three glimpses down on the symposium schedule. They form one part of a triangle; the other corners being me, and the place I call home.

JOHN WAKEMAN

The Head of Orpheus

The head of Orpheus
sailed out to sea,
mum in the hiss of the waves
but humming inside itself
to numb
the ache in the severed heart.

Fishes nibbled the streaming eyes,
they swallowed the silver tongue
but the pumping brain sang on,
past mermaids tidying their rocks,
past men on rafts, past continents,
remembering.

Remembering how once
mountains erupted when he touched his lyre,
rolled on their backs like puppies:
thousands died.
The head laughed.
Eurydice.

Remembering how once the king of hell,
hearing him sing, bawled like a bull
and tupped Persephone,
immediately, across her throne,
in front of all the dead.
The head laughed.

Remembering how the king,
his crown on crooked, panting,
sent for Eurydice and set them free,

gasping out warnings,
and looking round for more.
The head laughed.

Remembering how her bare feet sounded
behind him on the sandy path.
He sang away his secrets to her,
remember?
Climbing and singing
up to the hole of light.

He touched on the mechanics of metre,
the mathematics of rhyme,
the plangent chords that cover up wrong notes,
and how to tear the flimsy hearts of men,
make beasts of gods,
teach dreams to animals.

The head remembered how her soft feet faltered,
her soft hands shut his singing mouth
and turned him to her in the growing light.
Eurydice.
The skull laughed, floating down,
and went on singing.

After Orpheus lost Eurydice for the second and final time,
he wandered off into exile and encountered a band of
randy Thracian women. Orpheus was scarcely in the
mood for that class of thing, and this so irritated them that they
tore him to pieces. They tossed his head, still calling the name
of Eurydice, into the river of Hebrus, which presumably would
have carried it down to the sea.

This is obviously a poem about poetry, or about art in general,
about the ruthlessness of art, the lies it tells, its indomitability.

I think it works well in terms of rhyme, assonance and so on. When I wrote it, forty years ago, a friend said it was a breakthrough for me in formal terms and I'm afraid that, in those terms, I haven't bettered it yet.

EAMONN WALL

Four Stern Faces / South Dakota

I was living in a bedsit in Donnybrook
when John Lennon was shot outside the
Dakota apartment building in New York
and that's what I'm thinking this morning
piloting my family through the hollow
darkness on Iron Mountain Road, trespassing
on the holy ground of the Lakota nation.

Four stern faces in the distance address
me and when I get stuck after rattling off
Washington & Lincoln I call on my son to
fill-in the blanks and wonder how the hell
will I pass the civics test when I apply
for citizenship. I could tell you all
about Allen Ginsberg & Adrienne Rich
but presidents, state capitols and amendments
to the constitution would snooker me,
and I get the feeling the I.N.S. doesn't care
too much for postmodern American poetry.
My daughter belongs to the woods—mosses,
pine needles, slow moving light and shade,
a bright face in the back of the car
breathing a fantastic language, this
slow mid-morning pilgrimage I drive
my loved ones forward and climbing.

When Lennon was dying I was typing
the forms to come to America: on this
journey through the Sandhills—Irish sand
dunes without the sea—to the Black Hills
to wild flowers with names so gorgeous

I cannot bear to hear you say them.
Native people, 'Strawberry Fields Forever',
Ryan White dying in Indiana. My children
craving this just as the matchsticks and cats'
eyes on the Gorey road mesmerized them,
howling now for lunch. Here the light is
different, the evenings shorter, Gods are weeping.

And there's no escape from caring
or from history: to lie on high plains
prairie grasses, and Black Hills is to be
blown into their stories, drowned in
their summer rains. Just when I think I've
lost the Irish rings around the tree, I open
the door and find red clay stuck on the
tyres, the whole earth screaming, my children
breathing on the electric hairs above my collar.

Being woken one ordinary workday to Lennon
being dead, 'Imagine' on the radio, remembering
the grown-ups weeping in late November '63,
one morning in Dublin when it finally struck
that heroes are flowers constantly dying on
these black and holy hills we spend the years
wandering towards till light reveals a universe
beyond stony victorious faces bolted to a rock.

'Four Stern Faces/South Dakota' is a poetic/fictional recreation of a family road trip made in May 1994. We were living in Omaha, Nebraska, then and set out for the Black Hills in South Dakota. This was my first American road trip; my first journey into the American West; and, I still feel, a life-altering experience. Originally, I conceived of the poem's form as being shaped by tightly-crafted heroic couplets in homage to Alexander Pope, one of my heroes, and because I felt that the movement of the couplets would in some way convey the sense of wheels hitting the road in a rhythmic beat. However, I could not get things to work. Eventually, I went back to my more familiar mode: a narrative structure guided by voice, line-breaks, enjambment, assonance, and alliteration. Writing and drafting took about two years. An early version of the poem was published in *Here's Me Bus*, a New York magazine of Irish immigrant writing, with the revised version leading off my second book, *Iron Mountain Road* (Salmon, 1997).

I was awestruck by the deep beauty of the Black Hills: my first objective was to try to represent that sensation in the poem. Also, I knew that this simple journey with my wife and children had, in some deep way, provided me with a moment of pause, and an opportunity to graft the various parts of my own life to the landscape I was absorbing. And, to be on the holy ground of the Lakota nation where they believe humans first came into the world was a humbling experience. At the same time, I could notice how much this place belonged to the modern United States — Mount Rushmore's imperialist message had been placed at the center of things. On my return to Nebraska, I read volumes of history and literature related to the American West in general and to the Black Hills in particular; however, gaining a larger body of knowledge made writing the poem more difficult as there was so much to try to distill a lyric poem from. I was able to solve the problem by also writing a companion essay on the subject, 'The Black Hills, The Gorey Road' for *New Hibernia Review*.

In addition to the family road trip and the going into a new place, the poem tries to trace something of the immigrant world — one that forges connections with new places while, at the same time, asking the immigrant to re-imagine links to where he/she was born. By focusing on a particular family, I wanted the reader to see that immigrants are as human as people born in the USA. And, I sought to pay homage to the Lakota.

Alter Ego Quasimodo

I began writing the poem I would eventually simply call 'Q' when I was in my early twenties, giving it a twenty five year gestation period. The character of 'Q' himself emerged from a feverish mind in the course of the then numerous 'flare-ups' of an unusual disorder — I had suffered from Still's Disease, a rare variety of Rheumatoid Arthritis since the age of twelve. When the disease was active it gave me a very high fever twice a day, morning and evening as regular as daylight itself, as well as the more usual joint destruction. The treatment in those early years was very high doses of steroids which caused changes in body shape and psychology. Ultimately the joint-destruction resulted in hip replacements by the time I was thirty:

> Q conspires with god
> who appears in a green
> gown & wears latex.
> He leaves no forensics.
>
> Scalpel, he says.
> Q says: Say please.
> Clamp, he says.
> Say please.
> Chainsaw.

I was trying to express the strange state of mind that emerges from a combination of pain, fever and powerful drugs. So Q is the mind, a petulant, sarcastic, truculent alter ego. The body is an external object to that mind and Q holds it in a kind of studied contempt, though he is, of course, irrevocably and painfully attached to it:

Q is for half-made
self-made half-man
half-man half-hearted
a fine half.

Q's continual punning (on his name, for example) is a kind of distancing device. He jokes about the value of suffering ("Pain maketh the man"); religion ("Q meets The Good Cripple … Into each life,/And we all have our cross…Q guts him/with a boning knife"); the sexuality of the chronically ill ("Q's whiskers/frisk the brown-eyed nurse"); the slow destruction of the body that the condition entails ("Give me back my bones,/skin is nothing/but something to go out in"); the effects of the drugs ("His mushroom skin,/the bloat, the steroid moonskin"); and along the way takes in sly references to whatever his author was reading at the time — "I hate that vulgar crowd, / but I whistle at virgins" is a sly nod to Horace's *Odi profanum vulgus,* for example.

The poem would eventually be published in The SHOp in 2003 and in my second collection of poems *Fahrenheit Says Nothing To Me**. It is quite different to the more conventional structures, subjects and language of my first collection. In tone and structure it is much closer to 'Job in Heathrow', an equally long poem in *Ghost Estate* — I wanted to leave 'Q' unpunctuated like the poems in that collection, but courage failed me in the end. Both are what I call 'voice poems', with identifiable speakers. Both employ irony and quotation. But aside from these elements, 'Q' is an expression of the despair of the chronic sufferer and the dehumanised degradation of the medicalised life:

Into the spare room
of aspirants,
the transplant hearts,

kidneys, livers, eyes,
such delicate valves
& bivalves & molluscs,
the plastic hips & knees,
sub specie sterile.

Q comes in
& pokes around,
& sneezes.

Naughty naughty Mr Q,
sneezing spreads germs.
Haven't you ever heard
of handkerchiefs?

God chalks it down to Q,
another black one,
a mortaller,
because he meant it.

No pleading please,
no insanity
in this jurisdiction.
What you did was wrong,
naughty naughty Mr Q.

I believe in one god
                says Q,
who made me what I am.
        The bastard knew,
                he knew,
what I would turn into.
Take it up with god.

      So sue, says god,

I got it covered.

    & Q sued
    & lost.

And Q, by the way is short for Quasimodo, the hunchback found
on Quasimodo Sunday and raised in Notre Dame Cathedral. It
translates as something like 'as if', but 'quasi' can mean 'partly'
or 'half'. I also read it as 'misshapen':

        Q is for half-made
        self-made half-man
        half-man half-hearted
        a fine half.

        Quasi-fashionable
        quasi-made
        queasy Q.

        Half-a-leg is better
        than no leg,
        half a heart follows.

        Half way up
        he is neither
        up nor down,
        but uppers & downers help.

Pioneer

The last memories of her husband have been sewn
into a quilt which barely warms her nights.
After bad dreams, their son and daughter sleep
furled beneath small flags of nightshirt
and brushed cotton sleeve worn thin.
Four summers and their harsh winters
have passed since she marked his grave.
Her own parents write, begging her home,
begging, before the children run quite wild.
Formally, they offer a second cousin
with land near York, ask she seriously consider
this most suitable widower of some renown.
Their letters go unanswered.

She is loosely moored between two worlds,
anchored only by the children,
for all they have ever drunk is from the well of this place.
And what flows in her now
is rainwater, woodsmoke, silence reflected
on the lake surface; leaves turned,
hair snagged on briars. Stones. The small,
white feathers that line nests.
She is sung with fox bark and pheasant call.
Creatures roost in her thoughts, her days
are measured by the slink, the leap, the pounce,
the pitched balance of wings breaking into flight.
She too moves in feral ways.

And lavender soap on Sundays is a fine gauze veil,
though the men in church stare with downcast eyes,
she knows what it is they smell on her, and, wary of hunters,

is afraid. She lives where the long road from town
meets the trackless purple mountains. Some nights
leaning into the silver shadows at her door
she wonders who will come for her first.
For the quiet is also pregnant with alcohol and laughter,
with a swagger some miles off, and there are eyes
that watch from the mauve shadow inland;
if she stood still long enough,
had she interest in belonging,
they would take her as one of their own tribe.

All she has carved for herself is a small square of land,
free of chickweed and scutch-grass, soil abundant with seed.

The walls of my house are built of mountain sandstone, brown, white and mauve, mostly small, irregular rocks, long ago picked out of the fields hereabouts—but one or two are large, cut stones, corner stones the others rest on. So it is with 'Pioneer', a lot of my other poems are founded here. Looking back, I can see my second collection *Fur* grew out of 'Pioneer's' small square of land, its territory between the wild and the cultured world.

I wrote 'Pioneer' late one night after a particularly good poetry reading Joseph Woods and Tony Curtis gave in Clonmel. They were both so strong in their own voices, so certain. Listening to them, an urge rose in me, a need for self-articulation, to write something that really belonged to me. Defined me. I couldn't waste any more time.

I drove home down dark lanes, back to the old bone-setter's cottage I was renting on the side of Sliabh na mBan. It was a cold house, elementary and isolated. My life was fragile then. A lone parent of two young children, I was struggling to write my first novel, and working on a FÁS scheme as literature officer with the South Tipperary Arts Centre. But I was also living in an extraordinary place, where the fields ended and the high heather moors began. A quiet, still landscape where the details of nature were ripe for harvest. There was something about my mountain life which put me in mind of the pioneer women in America, and a question had risen up in me, what if one of those women were widowed, alone, would she stay?

When I got home that night, the poem was waiting for me. It wrote itself. 'Pioneer' remains a touchstone because it is veiled auto-biography. And because little has changed. My mother is still begging me back to civilization. I am still adrift between nature and culture, spirit and matter. As I begin to think about writing new poems for a third collection, 'Pioneer' is still calling me back to its territory. There's something the poem still wants me to resolve.

SANDRA ANN WINTERS

Death of Alaska

My white German Shepherd,
female ears tuned to sounds
I could not hear, disappeared the day my son left.

She must have heard him going;
he who cut me off like the sharp snip of scissors
against the papery peony stems.

She, my white cavalier, could not keep
me from the way he redrafted our love,
flinging himself, a young man now, into the universe.

For him, I canvassed the stars, glossed against a crêpe sky.
For her, I tramped through copsewood and brambles —
flashlight a-beam, calling her name.

But no staccato bark and no cantering boy returned,
and I stood alone in the spring cold midnight.

I was moved to write 'Death of Alaska' as a way to work through the grief of my son departing after eighteen years of learning and laughter at home. I used the disappearance of my beloved dog, who later appeared in our garden, having curled up in a corner and passed away at an old age, as the vehicle of parallel experience for my son going off to university.

Setting is usually another character in my poems, and the night setting here is true to my memory. I lived on a large farm that stretched out beneath dark, clear skies. I was walking across the pastures late at night calling for my dog, named Alaska by my ten-year-old son because she was white. The dark setting fosters the mystery of 'where is Alaska', as well as the mystery of how does a mother let go, how does anyone let go of a loved one. However, the dark night was clearly lit by stars, 'going' not a mystery at all.

I find poetry in the familiar peonies and brambles, flashlights, but also research unfamiliar words such as copsewood. I select my words for the rhythm, music, often using alliteration and tend to struggle with each word in the poem, choosing purposefully. The alliteration 'sharp snip of scissors' and the verb 'redrafted' were expressly chosen to evoke the way in which a young man declares his independence from a mother.

I chose 'canvassed', 'staccato', 'cantering', 'cold' for sound, and because each suggests the themes of searching and movement. Cantering was a familiar activity on the farm because my son grew up with a horse and often cantered across our fields.

The event weaves from a singular, personal experience to a universal theme of loss, a familiar experience of loved — ones moving on to a wider feeling of being part of a universal wisdom.

JOSEPH WOODS

Sailing to Hokkaido

After dinner
walk to the stern alone

and look out
for the time it takes

to discern two
darknesses from one.

Suiheisen was the line
where sky and sea met.

For two horizons,
sky and sea

land and sky
there are two words.

Tonight one darkness
overruns another.

There is no line between
the two. Walk back

to the palpable heartbeat
of a generator.

I wrote 'Sailing to Hokkaido' almost twenty years ago to the day and it was a kind of seminal poem for me and has stayed with me since. When I looked up my notebook of that time, I saw that I kept a diary of a journey I had made while living in Kyoto, Japan.

Having set out on a cargo ship, which also took passengers, from Maizuru on the western coast of Japan to the port of Otaru on the northern island of Hokkaido and thence north by a variety of trains, ostensibly to see the frozen sea of Okhotsk. I eventually reached the frozen sea, which was breaking up and from there I turned back.

I'd written a personal diary of the journey and then a draft of this poem appears on one page that reasonably resembles the published poem much later. I'd forgotten too that I was reading Pascal's *Pensées* (the Everyman edition introduced by Eliot which I still have, and missing one of its blue covers). Eliot mentions Pascal's journey in the dark night and of course there are marked passages.

> The whole visible world is only an imperceptible atom in the ample bosom of nature. No idea approaches it. We may enlarge our conceptions beyond all imaginable space ... the centre of which is everywhere, the circumference nowhere.

Clearly, reading Pascal influenced the sense of aloneness or the existential note in the poem, which was perhaps compounded by negotiating a new language. A language that had coinages for things we haven't named and visa versa. Only now I realise the positioning of the narrator is odd, if you want revelation on a boat journey, you'd probably head for the prow rather than the stern, to look backwards is to examine the past.

It's been pointed out to me that the title obviously echoes 'Sailing to an Island' or even 'Sailing to Byzantium' which set my heart racing, as no echo where none intended. Couplets are always good for breaking down concepts; two darknesses, two horizons, two words/worlds. I tend to write couplets when I'm trying to understand something for myself in the first place.

Three years later, John Banville published the poem in *The Irish Times,* and later again it seemed an appropriate title for my first book, which was full of journeys, arrivals and departures.

MACDARA WOODS

Fire And Snow And Carnevale

In winter fire is beautiful
beautiful like music
it lights the cave —
outside the people going home
drive slowly up the road — the strains
of phone-in Verdi on the radio
three hours back a fall of snow
sprinkled the furthest hill
where clouds have hung all winter

The day gets dark uneasy
dark and darker still
and you little son come home
riding the tail of the wind
in triumph — tall and almost ten
with confetti in your hair
home successful from the carnevale
with your two black swords
and your gold-handled knife

I feel the chill and hear
the absent sound of snow
when you come in —
white fantastic scorpions spit
in the fiery centre of the grate
plague pictures cauterised —
In winter fire is beautiful
and generous as music — may you
always come this safely home
in fire and snow and carnevale

S teering clear of mystique and mystification I would have to say that poems must be thematically congruent, however many variables insert themselves. Which is another way of saying that anything goes, so long as it goes along with everything else. A kind of controlled chaos.

Human interaction is like a street of busy motor traffic. a fluid series of accidents and collisions and explosions, that do not quite happen. Except that in poetical terms they do indeed happen, unnoticed for most of the time, leaving all the cab-drivers, pedestrians, cyclists wondering how they got to wherever they are. The poet, with luck, can identify some of the patterns, the forever unjoined dots, along the way.

My poem starts with Cold. Shrove Tuesday in Umbria, Lenten, and — because this belongs to all time — Seasonal period of abstinence coming up. My neighbour remarks: *In winter fire is beautiful.* I respond, *It lights the cave.* Which is as basic as it can get — all human history is contained in those four words, and after that the poem flows on its own narrative terms.

My son who has earlier gone to the local Carnevale, dressed as Zorro, is now returning from the Quest, like the Archetypal hero, in triumph, through the gothic darkness and danger.

And finally he finds me, sitting by the fire, allowing me to hear and feel momentarily the outside world he has travelled through. And, even though he has come safely home on this occasion, intimations of danger and harm remain in the pictures I see in the fire.

But then, again, in winter fire is beautiful not dangerous, and generous: like the phone-in Verdi, it keeps us warm and lights the cave. All I can add is what every parent has to in time: Go, go safely, and come back safe, and welcome home.

Within these parameters anything goes.

April 2ⁿᵈ 2016

VINCENT WOODS

Homeric Laughter

i.m. Sharon Lynch

That's what I heard, Sharon,
        ten years after your death;
Your beautiful, clear, singing laughter
        in my mind, in my dream, in me.
It filled the day with bird light
                with white hope.

You tell me in the dream
        you are going to be married;
you'll stand naked on your wedding dress
                for the ceremony;
you laugh, we both laugh,
        as we did when we were nineteen
and one louche Friday afternoon, for a dare —
                remember —
we went into a bridal shop,
        a posh one
on Stephen's Green, with Anne.

You were the bride-to-be, you said,
Anne was your bridesmaid,
I was the groom:
They looked me up and down

But I think they believed you,
        even when they asked when is the wedding
And you named a date not a month off;
        I could see their polite eye-masks
adding two and two and you and me

and getting a baby-on-the-way.

Bride and bridesmaid paraded in white dresses,
    flouncy, tapered, taffeta,
barefoot, the two of you barefoot,
twirling, tossing your hair,
    and we laughed and tried not to laugh
and the more we smothered it the more
    the mirrors brimmed with laughter;

'I like this one,' you'd say, 'what do you think —
    does it suit my eyes?
How much? Only 300. I'll take two!'

2

That was five years before you died.
Do you remember that last day?
How we meet by accident on Andrew Street —
You're off to France that evening
and we spend the afternoon in pubs and cafés,
drinking, talking, making love to life.

You tell me about your Christmas at home
    and what was said;
Your eyes fill up with tears,
    you smudge them half-away.

I walk you to the taxi rank on Aston Quay
And we kiss goodbye forever.

Three days later you're dead
    on a railway platform near Montpelier;
That fall from the barely moving train,

that fall through time.
A man watches your life leaving your eyes.
I overhear the news on a November seven bus —
        'Where did it happen?' one girl asks,
'In the South of France, they're bringing
        the body back next week.'

The body

I don't know how I knew it was you —
How could I not know?

And so

        The snow-covered midlands

The church with a dozen priests on the altar
(One says:
        'I remember when Sharon was a twinkle in her father's eye')

The nuns from your schooldays,
        Their calm excitement —
'with her boyfriend in the south of France.'

Denis is waiting in the snow by your grave,
        We hug and hold each other —
'You must meet,' you'd said, 'some day
        I know you two will meet.'

Your mother meets us at the door
        of their new house —
'Well Anne,' she says, 'a sad end to Sharon ...'

        I can't remember what we ate or drank.

That night, in Tullamore, I walk out on the frozen canal

3

I don't remember it till next day,
   watching the whitened landscape
     through the train window

Your dream, when we were nineteen,
   after a few joints,
the dream you laughed away
       but I knew it haunted you:

'I saw Jack Frost last night,' you said,
     'this sinister
     Jack Frost face
   looking in the window
     at me.

And I saw you walking on water — like Jesus.'

It was the Jesus bit we'd laugh about for months after,
But it wasn't funny, you said, it frightened you.

And now they're here, those two images,
    You in your snow-grave,
Me walking the canal water,
  those two images
       staring back at me
    on a train   on a train
      on a train

and you're gone, vanished out of life,
   and I can't tell you what I now know.

That same year as the wedding dress, remember,
   we read *The Dead* in college —

'snow is general all over Ireland'

4

Twenty years ago, twenty years

I've never visited your grave —
Some day I will,
but I think of you every time
　　I drive through that town,
every time I take a train south in France,
　　every snowfall

every dreamless night
　　listening for laughter,
the mirror silent
　　　　In my darkening room

It took me twenty years to write 'Homeric Laughter'. Such is poem-making. You must have patience to wait; trust to believe that word will come; will to work word and form.

Each poem is different and the way each poem comes to life is different. Yes, words to a page but the number of drafts will vary, the time between mind and pen will be different, the length you carry the seed of an idea before it forces through will never be the same.

'Homeric Laughter' is one of a small number of poems that I stored and built for years, then wrote with a sudden speed and clarity ('Famine Pit' is another). I seldom read it in public, though the poem takes on a whole other tone and power in its spoken form; and the few times I have read it brought music to the fore (Emer Mayock playing 'Midnight Water' after a reading in The Tyrone Guthrie Centre at Annaghmakerrig; Charlie McGettigan singing a song for his son Shane after a reading in the Dock in Carrick-On-Shannon, a song he said he hadn't been able to sing since Shane's young death).

I suppose this poem holds everything for me; the enduring power of love, the possibility of what we see beyond life and out of time, the power of laughter, the uncertainty of life, the fragility of the moment, the suddenness of the fall.

The grace of what is given in a glance.

When a poem is published it moves away from you, enters the world on its own terms. The young people in 'Homeric Laughter' live beyond time — no Tír na nÓg, though — in a place where the poem holds the spirit, and that is enough.

ENDA WYLEY

Magpie

for Freya Sirr

The day builds itself piece by piece;
the newt joins the owl, then the porcupine,
quince on its branch bends over a ruby ring,
colour seeping across the living room floor

until the jigsaw's yacht sails to its zebra end
and we go walking, your hand a small ball
in my palm poised to roll where any adventure lies,
hidden in parks, wild gardens, up doorsteps, behind pots.

Your eyes, beady berries on Raymond Street's trees,
see everything — and then, just there, muck-pie,
muck-pie, you call to the bird that tussles
with the daffodils, that pecks for sparkling light

like diamonds through the railings. Our day
building and renewing will not stop.
Blueberries devoured, cod stew and sleep
the warm milk of waking, later the afternoon

becoming a city of wooden blocks up to the ceiling —
only the great moon in the sky and the twinkling star
will drag you in song from your industry.
Then night has you nestling close to my neck,

your lips whispering the day's things softly.
Muck-pie, muck-pie, your little fingers pulling
at the jade on my chain, feel relentless to me
like the jay all ready to steal and fly away.

Becoming a mother for the first time surprised me. I had expected exhaustion — late nights, constants feeds, a whirl of changing nappies and a myriad of maternal anxieties. Yes, all these things — and much more — did happen. But strangely, in the midst of all these frantic musings and sleeplessness, I began to experience a peculiar and welcome calmness. Time slowed and I was surprised by the realisation that although our world had been turned upside down, joy had somehow defeated exhaustion. The precious moments spent with our baby became paramount.

It was impossible to achieve long stretches of writing during these months but I did manage to observe closely the daily rituals and simple patterns that made up our daughter's day and now and then I would reach for a notebook to scribble down my thoughts. I wanted to record the early periods of babyhood which I knew would be forgotten about as soon as the next stage of her development took off. Poetry is, after all, the netting of a moment before life moves on.

What grew from this notebook was a series of poems about motherhood — 'Magpie' just being one of them.

It is ten years later and recently I found that green notebook again — poems half-formed between jottings about feeds and sleep times. They depict a world far removed from my own now. But looking back on them, I am happy that these poems record the objects and simple happenings that were integral to the first few months of Freya's life — the blueberry snacks, the feeding, the sprawling jigsaw, the jade stone which she liked to clutch as a talisman before she napped, the afternoon walks and the magpie which soared as a *Muck-pie* from her little lips.

In the early years of motherhood I felt free to write again, discovered that the joy of parenting is as valid a poetic theme as any other. For there are no rules to writing and poetry can be about anything you chose — even a baby and a magpie.

BIOGRAPHICAL NOTES

Graham Allen is a Professor in the School of English, UCC. He has published poetry in numerous journals. He won the 2010 Listowel Single Poem Prize and has been shortlisted for a number of awards including The Crashaw Prize in 2014 and the Strong/Shine Prize in 2015. His collections *The One That Got Away* (2014) and *The Madhouse System* (2016), along with his on-going epoem *Holes,* are published by New Binary Press.

Tara Bergin was born in Dublin and presently lives in North Yorkshire. Her debut collection of poems, *This is Yarrow* (Carcanet Press, 2013) won the Seamus Heaney Prize for Poetry. She was chosen as one of the Poetry Society's Next Generation Poets in 2014.

Eavan Boland was born in Dublin in 1944, and studied in Ireland, London and New York. She is currently Mabury Knapp Professor in the Humanities at Stanford University, California. Her many volumes of poetry include *The Journey and Other Poems* (1987), *Night Feed* (1994), *The Lost Land* (1998), *Code* (2001) and *A Woman Without a Country* (2014). *New Collected Poems* was published by Carcanet Press in 2005.

Dermot Bolger is one of Ireland's best-known writers and was, for many years, one of its most innovative literary publishers. A poet, playwright and novelist, he was born in 1959 in Dublin where he still lives. He has won many awards for his writing and his novels have been translated into numerous languages. His poetry collections include *The Venice Suite* (2012), commemorating his late wife Bernie, while *That Which Is Suddenly Precious: New and Selected Poems* was published in 2015.

Pat Boran (See 'About the Editors', p. 318)

Eva Bourke was born in Germany but has lived in Galway for many years. She has published five books of poems, *piano* (Dedalus Press, 2011) being the most recent. She has edited many books and co-edited *Landing Places: Immigrant Poets in Ireland* (Dedalus Press, 2010). She teaches Irish literature in Europe and is currently editing a translation of the poet Friedrich Hoelderlin. She is co-editor, with Vincent Woods, of fermata, Vincent Woods fermata, an anthology of writing inspired by music (Artisan House Editions, 2016). She is a member of Aosdána.

Heather Brett is a writer and artist, born in Newfoundland and long since living in Ireland. Writer-in-Residence for several counties, she is founder/editor of Windows Publications (founded in 1992) and has edited over 40 anthologies. She has published four poetry collections, the first of which won the Brendan Behan Memorial Prize. Her most recent, *Witness*, was published in 2015.

Paddy Bushe was born in Dublin in 1948. A bilingual poet, he has written seven collections of poems in Irish and English, as well as three books of translations. *To Ring in Silence: New and Selected Poems* was published by Dedalus Press in 2008. His latest collection is *On a Turning Wing* (Dedalus Press, 2016).

Rosemary Canavan was born in Scotland in 1949. She was brought up in the North of Ireland, and after forty years in Cork now lives in France. Her first collection of poems, *The Island*, was shortlisted for the Vincent Buckley Poetry Prize (University of Melbourne, Australia) and her second, *Trucker's Moll*, appeared in 2009. Other publications include children's books, translations of French short stories and anthologies. She is currently completing a third collection of poetry, and a biography.

Moya Cannon was born in County Donegal and lives in Dublin. *Keats Lives* (Carcanet Press, Manchester) is her fifth collection of poetry. She was a winner of the Brendan Behan Award and the Laurence O'Shaughnessy Award. She has been Editor of *Poetry Ireland Review* and was 2011 Heimbold Professor of Irish Studies at Villanova University P.A. She is a member of Aosdána.

Ciaran Carson (*b.* Belfast, 1948) is a poet, translator, essayist, traditional musician and novelist. He is Professor of Poetry and Director of the Seamus Heaney Centre at Queen's University, Belfast. He has published fourteen collections of poetry, including *Collected Poems* (The Gallery Press, 2008) and *Until Before After* (The Gallery Press, 2010) while his translations include *The Inferno of Dante Aligheri* (2002), *The Táin* and *From Elsewhere* (2014). His prose works include *Last Night's Fun* (1996), a study of Irish traditional music, and the memoir *The Star Factory* (1997). Awards include The T.S. Eliot and the Oxford Weidenfeld Translation Prizes.

Paul Casey was born in Cork and grew up in Zambia and South Africa. *The Lamas Hireling*, a film on the poem by Ian Duhig, premiered in Berlin in 2010. He is the founder of the Ó Bhéal reading series in Cork. *Virtual Tides,* his second collection, was published by Salmon Poetry in 2016.

Philip Casey was born in 1950 to Irish parents in London, raised in Co. Wexford and has long since lived in Dublin. A poet and fiction writer, he has published three acclaimed novels *(The Bann River Trilogy)*, as well as *Tried and Sentenced: Selected Poems,* and short fiction for children, including *Coupla*, all of these now available from eMaker Editions. He is a member of Aosdána.

Sarah Clancy is an award-winning page and performance poet from Galway. She has published three collections of poetry, *Stacey and the Mechanical Bull* (Lapwing Press, 2011), *Thanks for Nothing, Hippies* (Salmon Poetry, 2012) and *The Truth and Other Stories* (Salmon Poetry, 2014). She is on Twitter @sarahmaintains.

Michael Coady was born in Carrick-on-Suir in 1939. *Oven Lane* (1987) and *All Souls* (1997), published by The Gallery Press, are among his numerous publications. His awards include the Lawrence O'Shaughnessy Award for Poetry. He is a member of Aosdána and a frequent contributor to RTÉ Radio.

Enda Coyle-Greene has published widely and is also a frequent contributor to programmes on RTÉ radio. Her first collection, *Snow Negatives,* won the Patrick Kavanagh Award in 2006 and was published by Dedalus Press in 2007. Her second collection, *Map of the Last,* also from Dedalus, was published in 2013.

Tony Curtis was born in Dublin in 1955. *Approximately in the Key of C* (Arc Publications, 2015) is his tenth collection. He travels widely, reading from his work and conducting poetry workshops, in schools, prisons and other institutions. He has been awarded the Irish National Poetry Prize and is a member of Aosdána.

Pádraig J. Daly was born in Dungarvan, Co. Waterford in 1943 and works as an Augustinian priest in Dublin city. He has published numerous collections of poetry, including *The Last Dreamers: New and Selected Poems* (Dedalus Press, 1999). He also translates from the Irish and the Italian. His translation of a poem of Edoardo Sanguineti's features on the cover of *The FGS Book of Italian Poetry.* His most recent book of poems is *God in Winter* (Dedalus Press, 2015)

Kathy D'Arcy is a Cork-born poet whose collections are *Encounter* (Lapwing, 2010) and *The Wild Pupil* (Bradshaw Books, 2012). In 2013 she was awarded an Arts Council Literature Bursary, and in 2014 an Irish Research Council Award for a PhD in Creative Writing. She has worked as a doctor, a youth worker and with homeless teenagers and families in crisis. She was 2016 editor of the *Cork Literary Review* and of *Rhyme Rag,* an online poetry journal for young people. See: *www.kathydarcy.com*

Michael Davitt was born in Cork. He was founder of *Innti*, the Irish language poetry magazine. He published numerous poetry collections and worked as a Director and Broadcaster with RTÉ. (The translator Moira Sweeney is a broadcaster, artist and educator. She has produced and directed documentaries and studio programmes for RTÉ, TG4, BBC and Channel 4.)

Gerald Dawe was born in Belfast and lives in Dublin. He has published eight collections of poetry with The Gallery Press, including *The Lundys Letter*, awarded the Macaulay Fellowship in Literature, and, more recently, *Selected Poems* (2012) and *Mickey Finn's Air* (2014). He is currently a visiting scholar at Pembroke College, Cambridge.

John F. Deane was born on Achill Island in 1943. He founded Poetry Ireland and the Poetry Ireland Review. He is a member of Aosdána and the Teilhard de Chardin fellow in Catholic Studies, teaching poetry for the fall semester, 2016, in Loyola University Chicago. His latest collection is *Semibrev* (Carcanet Press, 2015). A faith and poetry memoir, *Give Dust a Tongue*, was published by Columba in 2015.

Mary Dorcey was born in Dublin. Her poetry collections include *Kindling* (1989), *Moving into the Space Cleared by Our Mothers* (1991), *The River That Carries Me* (1995), and *Perhaps the Heart is Constant after All* (2012). Her fiction includes *A Noise from the Woodshed: Short Stories* (1989) and the novel *Biography of Desire* (1997). The recipient of the 1990 Rooney Prize for Literature, she is a Research Associate at Trinity College Dublin and writer-in-residence at the Centre for Gender and Women's Studies. She is a member of Aosdána.

Theo Dorgan is a Cork-born poet, novelist, essayist and broadcaster. His most recent collection of poems, *Nine Bright*

Shiners (Dedalus Press 2014), won the Irish Times/Poetry Now Award for best collection in 2015. Following *Barefoot Souls* (Arc 2015), his latest translations of Syrian poet Maram al-Masri are published as *Liberty Walks Naked* (Southword Editions, 2017). He is a member of Aosdána.

Cal Doyle lives in Cork. His poetry has appeared in a various journals and anthologies, including *Southword, Gorse,* and *The Burning Bush 2*. He has read as part of Poetry Ireland's Introductions Series and is the poetry editor for *wordlegs* and *The Weary Blues*.

Martina Evans was born in Burnfort in Co. Cork. Poet and Novelist. *Burnfort, Las Vegas,* her most recent collection of poems, was shortlisted for the Irish Times Poetry Now Award in 2015. She teaches at Goldsmith College in London.

John FitzGerald was awarded the 2014 Patrick Kavanagh Poetry Prize for an unpublished collection of poems. He was shortlisted for the 2015 Hennessy New Irish Writing Award. He is currently University Librarian at University College Cork and lives with his family on a farm in Lissarda.

Gabriel Fitzmaurice was born in Moyvane, Co Kerry, in 1952. He has published more than forty books of poetry, fiction, memoir, writing for children and translation. He has edited books on the life and work of John B. Keane and Brian McMahon and was chairman of Listowel Writers' Week for eleven years. He broadcasts frequently on RTÉ Radio. Among his recent publications is *Will You Be My Friend? New and Selected Poems* (Liberties Press, 2016).

Anne-Marie Fyfe's fifth collection is *House of Small Absences* (Seren, 2015). Born in Cushendall, County Antrim, she works as an arts organiser in London where she has run Coffee-House

Poetry's Troubadour readings & classes since 1997, is Poetry Co-ordinator for the John Hewitt Summer School in Armagh, and is former chair of the UK's Poetry Society.

Matthew Geden was born in England and has lived in Kinsale since 1990. One of the founders of Cork's SoundEye International Poetry Festival, his collections include *Swimming to Albania* (Bradshaw Books, 2009) and *The Place Inside* (Dedalus Press, 2012).

Rody Gorman was born in Dublin in 1960 and lives on the Isle of Skye. His most recent collections are *Ceangailte* (Coiscéim, 2011) and *Beartan Briste* (Cape Breton University Press, 2011).

Mark Granier is a Dublin-based writer and photographer. His fourth collection of poetry is *Haunt* (Salmon Poetry, 2015). Prizes and awards include the Vincent Buckley Poetry Prize in 2004 and a Patrick and Katherine Kavanagh Fellowship in 2011. He currently teaches Creative Writing for UCD's Adult Education programme and at The Irish Writers' Centre.

Vona Groarke has published ten titles with The Gallery Press, including seven poetry collections, the latest being *Selected Poems* (2016). Her most recent publication is a book-length essay on art frames, *Four Sides Full*. Her poems have appeared in *The New Yorker*, *Threepenny Review*, *Poetry* and *Poetry Review*. A former editor of *Poetry Ireland Review*, current selector for the UK's Poetry Book Society and a member of Aosdána, she teaches poetry in the Centre for New Writing at the University of Manchester.

Kerry Hardie has published seven collections of poetry, two novels, and a *Selected Poems* (The Gallery Press, 2011). She has also written a drama for radio with Olivia O'Leary, RTÉ 2015.

Maurice Harmon is the leading scholar of his generation in the field of Anglo-Irish literature. He has written bibliographical guides to headline studies of Sean Ó Faoláin, Austin Clarke, Thomas Kinsella and others. His own poetry collections include *When Love is Not Enough: New and Selected Poems* (Salmon Poetry, 2010) and *Loose Connections* (2012). *Hoops of Holiness* (2016) is his latest volume. He is Professor Emeritus of English Literature at University College Dublin.

James Harpur is the author of five books of poems, including *Angels and Harvesters* (Anvil Press, 2012), a PBS Recommendation and shortlisted for the Irish Times Poetry Prize. He won the British National Poetry Prize in 1995 and has been awarded bursaries by The Arts Council, the Eric Gregory Trust and the Society of Authors. Non-fiction books include *Love Burning in the Soul,* an introduction to Christian mystics. He lives in West Cork and is a member of Aosdána.

Michael Hartnett was born in West Limerick in 1941 and died in Dublin in 1999. The Gallery Press publish his major collections, including *A Farewell to English, A Necklace of Wrens* (poems in Irish with English translations), *The Killing of Dreams, Selected Poems* and his acclaimed trilogy of translations of the 17th century poets O Bruadair, Haicéad and O Rathaille. *Collected Poems* was published by The Gallery Press in 2001.

Eleanor Hooker lives in Co. Tipperary and is a nurse and midwife by profession. She studied for an MPhil in Creative Writing at Trinity College, Dublin. *The Shadow Owner's Companion* (Dedalus Press, 2012), her debut collection, was followed in 2016 by *A Tug of Blue.* She is Programme Curator for the Dromineer Literary Festival and helm for Lough Derg RNLI Lifeboat. See: *www.eleanorhooker.com*

Breda Joy was born in Killarney. She is a poet, short story writer and historian. Widely published, she was awarded an MPhil in Creative Writing from Trinity College, Dublin. *Hidden Kerry* (Mercier Press) was published in 2014. A winner of the Provincial Journalist of the Year award, she works with *Kerry's Eye* newspaper.

Patrick Kehoe was born in Enniscorthy, Co. Wexford in 1957 and is a poet and journalist. His debut collection of poems, *Its Words You Want,* was published by Salmon Poetry and the follow-up, *The Cask of Moonlight,* by Dedalus Press in 2014.

Brendan Kennelly *(b.* Ballylongford, Co. Kerry, 1936) is a poet, anthologist, novelist and Professor Emeritus of English Literature at Trinity College, Dublin. One of Ireland's most popular poets, he has published numerous collections of poetry, among them *The Book of Judas,* which topped the Irish best sellers list in 1991. His recent books include *The Essential Brendan Kennelly: Selected Poems* (2011) and *Guff* (2003), all published by Bloodaxe Books.

Helen Kidd. Poet and Editor of *The Virago Book of Love Poetry.* She teaches at Ruskin College Oxford where she is Director of Creative Writing. Her collection of poetry, *Blue Weather,* is published in Ireland by Bradshaw Books.

Noel King was born and lives in Tralee, Co Kerry. His poetry collections are published by Salmon: *Prophesying the Past,* (2010), *The Stern Wave* (2013) and *Sons* (2015). He has edited more than fifty books by others (Doghouse Books, 2003–2013). A short story collection, *The Key Signature & Other Stories* is forthcoming from Liberties Press.

Thomas Kinsella *(b.* Inchicore, Dublin, 1928) is a poet, translator and editor. His extensive translations from the Irish include *The Táin* (Dolmen, 1969 and Oxford, 1970) and *An Duanaire: 1600-1900, Poems of the Dispossessed* (1981), edited by Seán Ó Tuama. *Butcher's Dozen* (1972), his response to the Widgery Report into the shootings of Bloody Sunday, lead to his Peppercanister series of pamphlets. *Collected Poems* was published by Carcanet Press in 1998 and updated in 2001.

Jessie Lendennie is a poet, editor and publisher of Salmon Poetry. In early 2016 she edited the anthology, *Even the Daybreak: 35 Years of Salmon Poetry.*

John Liddy is a Limerick-born poet and founding editor of *The Stony Thursday Book*. His books include *The Angling Cot* (Beaver Row Press, 1991). He teaches at the University of Madrid in Spain.

Alice Lyons' latest collection *The Breadbasket of Europe* was published in 2016 by Veer Books, London. A recipient of the Patrick Kavanagh Award and an Ireland Chair of Poetry bursary, Lyons was a 2015/16 Fellow in Poetry at the Radcliffe Institute for Advanced Study, Harvard University.

Aifric Mac Aodha's first collection, *Gabháil Syrinx* (The Capture of Syrinx) was published by An Sagart in 2010. She is a former editor of *Comhar*, and the current Irish language poetry editor of *The Stinging Fly, gorse* and Poetry Ireland's *Trumpet*.

Jennifer Matthews is originally from the US but has lived and worked in Ireland and become an Irish citizen. She is founding editor of the journal *Long Story, Short*. She has published poems in anthologies that include *The Stinging Fly, Cork Literary Review, Poetry Salzburg* and *The Irish Examiner* and *Landing Places: Immigrant Poets in Ireland* (Dedalus Press, 2010). *Rootless, a* chapbook, was published by Smithereens in 2015.

John McAuliffe is a poet and co-director of the University of Manchester's Centre for New Writing. His books include *A Better Life* (2002), *Next Door* (2007), *Of All Places* (2011), and

The Way In (2015), all from The Gallery Press. He is poetry critic with *The Irish Times*.

Joan McBreen divides her time between Tuam and Renvyle, Co. Galway. She has published four poetry collections, and edited two anthologies. Her CD, *The Mountain Ash in Connemara*, with music by composer Glen Austin, performed by the RTÉ Contempo String Quartet, appeared in 2014. A broadside, with artist Margaret Irwin West and print-maker Mary Plunkett was published by Artisan House in 2015 and short-listed for the National Fine Art and Print Competition 'Legacy'.

Thomas McCarthy is a poet, editor and literary critic. *Pandemonium*, his latest collection of poems, is published by Carcanet Press in 2016. He is a member of Aosdána.

Philip McDonagh was born in Dublin in 1952. He has served as ambassador in India, the Holy See, Finland, Russia, and (currently) the OSCE in Vienna. He has published four collections of poetry, including *The Song the Oriole Sang* (Dedalus Press, 2010) and a translation of Nikolay Gumilyov's *Gondla* (2016).

Afric McGlinchey's awards include the Hennessy Poetry Award, Northern Liberties Prize (USA) and Poets Meet Politics prize. She was selected as one of Ireland's 'rising poets' for issue 118 of *Poetry Ireland Review*. Her second collection, *Ghost of the Fisher Cat* (Salmon), was nominated for the 2016 Forward Prize. See: *www.africmcglinchey.com*

Iggy McGovern is a Fellow Emeritus of the School of Physics at Trinity College Dublin. He has published three collections of poetry, *The King of Suburbia* and *Safe House* (both from Dedalus Press) and *A Mystic Dream of 4* (Quaternia Press). He has edited *20/12: Irish Poets Respond to Science in 12 Lines*.

Medbh McGuckian was born in 1950 in Belfast where she continues to live. She has been Writer-in-Residence at Queen's University, Belfast, the University of Ulster, Coleraine, and Trinity College, Dublin, and was Visiting Fellow at the University of California, Berkeley. Prizes include England's National Poetry Competition, The Cheltenham Award, The Rooney Prize, the Bass Ireland Award for Literature and The Forward Prize for Best Poem. She received the American Ireland Fund Literary Award in 1998. She has published more than a dozen collections of poetry — most recently *The High Caul Cap* (2012) and *Blaris Moor* (2015) — all from The Gallery Press. She is a member of Aosdána.

John Mee won the Patrick Kavanagh Award 2015 and the Fool for Poetry Chapbook Competition 2016. His pamphlet, *From the Extinct,* is published by Southword Editions (2017). Poems have appeared in numerous journals including *The Rialto, Prelude, The SHOp, Poetry on the Buses* (London), *Cyphers, Southword* etc. He is a professor of law at University College Cork.

Paula Meehan was born in Dublin in 1955. A poet and playwright, she has received numerous awards for her writing — including the Martin Toonder Award and the Lawrence O'Shaughnessy Award for Poetry — and was Ireland Professor of Poetry, 2013–2016. Her latest collection of poems is *Geomantic* (Dedalus Press, 2016). She is a member of Aosdána.

John Moriarty (1938–2007) was born in Leitrim Hill, Moyvane, Co. Kerry and was a poet and mystic whose books were regularly on the Irish bestsellers lists. Among the best known titles are *Nostos* (Lilliput Press) and *What the Curlew Said,* a posthumously published memoir.

Aidan Murphy was born in Cork but has lived much of his life in London. His books include *The Way the Money Goes* (Allison and Busby/Raven Arts Press) and *Small Sky, Big Change* (Raven, 1989). His latest collection is *Wrong Side of Town* (Dedalus Press, 2015). He received the Patrick and Katherine Kavanagh fellowship for poetry in 2012.

Gerry Murphy was born and lives in Cork. A prolific poet, his poems have also been set to music and performed, to critical acclaim, as the stage show *The People's Republic of Gerry Murphy*, by Crazy Dog Audio Theatre. Books include, *End of Part One, New and Selected Poems* (Dedalus Press, 2006). *Muse*, his latest, was published by Dedalus Press in 2015.

Madelaine Nerson Mac Namara was born in London, grew up in Paris, and has lived in Cork since 1967. Her work has been published in a variety of literary magazines and anthologies. She was guest reader at Ó Bhéal, Cork in 2016. *The Riddle of Waterfalls* (Bradshaw Books, 2015) was shortlisted for the Strong / Shine Awards 2016.

Caitríona Ní Chléirchín, originally from Emyvale, Co. Monaghan, is a poet, critic and Irish-language lecturer at University College Dublin. Her academic and scholarly articles have been widely published and her debut collection of poems, *Crithloinnir* (Coscéim, 2010), won first prize in that year's Oireachtas competition for new writers.

Nuala Ní Chonchúir, a.k.a Nuala O'Connor, has published four short story collections, three novels and three poetry collections. Her third novel, *Miss Emily* (Penguin USA & Canada, & Sandstone UK), about the poet Emily Dickinson and her Irish maid, was shortlisted for the Bord Gáis Energy Novel of the Year 2015. See: *www.nualanichonchuir.com*.

Eiléan Ní Chuileanáin was born in Cork in 1942, educated there and at Oxford. She is a Fellow and Professor (emeritus)

School of English, Trinity College Dublin. Her many collections of poetry include *The Sun-fish* (The Gallery Press, 2009) which won the 2010 Griffin International Poetry Prize. Her most recent collection is *The Boys of Bluehill* (The Gallery Press, 2015). A founding editor of *Cyphers*, she is a member of Aosdána.

Ailbhe Ní Ghearbhuigh was born in Kerry. In 2012 her poem 'Deireadh na Feide' won the O'Neill Poetry Prize. 'Filleadh ar an gCathair' was chosen as Ireland's EU Presidency poem in 2013 and was shortlisted in 2015 for RTE's 'A Poem for Ireland'. Her first collection, *Péacadh*, was published by Coiscéim in 2008. *Tost agus Allagar* (2016) is the title of her latest.

Áine Ní Ghlinn is a children's writer, poet, broadcaster and lecturer, with some 28 books to her name. She has won several awards for poetry, drama and fiction for children and young adults. These include Irish Language Children's Book of the Year, the CBI Fiction Award and Literacy Association Book of the Year.

Doireann Ní Ghríofa is a bilingual writer whose work has appeared in *The Irish Times, The Stinging Fly, Poetry* and elsewhere. Among her awards are the Ireland Chair of Poetry bursary and the Rooney Prize for Irish Literature. Her most recent book — and her English-language debut — is *Clasp* (Dedalus Press, 2015) which was shortlisted for the Irish Times Poetry Award.

Mary Noonan is a Cork-born poet and academic. Her debut collection of poems, *The Fado House* (Dedalus Press), was awarded the Listowel Writers' Week Poetry Collection Prize in 2010. She teaches French at University College Cork.

Julie O'Callaghan was born in Chicago and has lived in Ireland for many years. Her most recent publication is *Tell Me This Is Normal: New and Selected Poems* published by Bloodaxe Books in 2008.

Eugene O'Connell (See 'About the Editors', p. 318)

John O'Donnell was born in 1960. He has published three collections of poetry, *Some Other Country* (Bradshaw Books, 2002), *Icarus Sees his Father Fly* and *On Water*, both from Dedalus Press. He has received a Hennessy award for poetry, the Ireland Funds Prize and the Seacat National Poetry Award. He is a Senior Counsel in Dublin.

Mary O'Donnell is a poet, novelist and short story writer. Her books include the poetry collection *These April Fevers* (Arc Publications, 2015), and the novel *Where They Lie* (New Island, 2014). She is a former presenter of *The Poetry Programme* on RTÉ Radio 1 and a member of Aosdána.

Bernard O'Donoghue was born in the townland of Knockduff, near Cullen, North West Cork, in 1945. He has published eight books of poetry including *Gunpowder* (1995) which won the Whitbread Prize, and *Selected Poems* (Faber, 2008). He has written a study of Seamus Heaney, and translated *Sir Gawain and the Green Knight* (Penguin, 2006). He is Fellow Emeritus at Wadham College, Oxford and adjunct Professor of English Literature at University College Cork.

Liz O'Donoghue is a poet and film-maker. She was producer/director of the film anthology *In the Hands of Erato* (2003). Her books include *Waitress at the Banquet* (1995) and *Train to Gorey* (Arlen House, 2009). She translated the poetry of the Lithuanian poet Sigitas Parulskis as part of the Cork European City of Culture Translation Series 2005. Her film *Murphy's Wall* was screened at the Cork Film Festival in 2011.

Mary O'Donoghue was born in 1975, grew up in Co. Clare and now lives in Boston, Massachussetts where she is associate professor of English at Babson College. She has published two collections of poems, *Tulle* (Salmon Poetry, 2001) and *Among These Winters* (Dedalus Press, 2007), and her poems have appeared widely in Irish and international journals and anthologies. Her novel, *Before the House Burns,* was published by Lilliput Press in 2010.

Sheila O'Hagan has received many awards for her poetry, including the Goldsmith Award 1991, the Patrick Kavanagh Award and the Hennessy/Sunday Tribune Award for New Irish Poet of the Year. *The Peacock's Eye* and *The Troubled House,* along with a short story collection *Along the Liffey,* are published by Salmon.

Nessa O'Mahony is from Dublin. She has published four volumes of poetry, the most recent being *Her Father's Daughter* (Salmon Poetry, 2014). She has twice received Arts Council bursaries for literature, and is holder of a Simba Gill fellowship.

Mary O'Malley was brought up in Connemara and has lived and taught in Portugal and the US. She is the author of eight collections of poetry, including *Playing The Octopus* (Carcanet Press, 2016). She is working on a memoir of childhood, as well as essays on place. She is a member of Aosdána and has won a number of awards for her poetry. She writes for RTÉ Radio and broadcasts her work regularly. She was the 2016 Arts Council Writer–in-Residence at University of Limerick.

Leanne O'Sullivan was born in Cork in 1983. Her books, which include *Waiting for my Clothes* and *The Mining Road,* published by Bloodaxe Books, have won numerous awards. She teaches creative writing at University College Cork.

Karl Parkinson is a writer from inner-city Dublin. *The Blocks* (New Binary Press, 2016) is his début novel, while his second collection of poems, *Butterflies of a Bad Summer,* was published in 2016 by Salmon Poetry. His work has appeared widely in anthologies. As a live performer, he has read at festivals throughout Ireland and abroad, and he is one half of the spoken word / electro music duo, The King Mob.

Paul Perry was born in Dublin in 1972. He has won the Hennessy New Irish Writer of the Year Award, the Listowel Prize for Poetry and has been a James Michener Fellow of Creative Writing at the University of Miami and a Camber Fellow of Poetry at the University of Houston. *Gunpowder Valentine: New and Selected Poems* (Dedalus Press, 2014) draws on three earlier collections. He teaches creative writing at Kingston University London and University College Dublin. He is a former Curator of Poetry Now at Mountains to Sea, dlr Book Festival.

Billy Ramsell was born in Cork in 1977 and educated at North Monastery and UCC. His work goes some way to bridging the gap between writing for the page and the stage. Dedalus has published his two collections to date, *Complicated Pleasures* (2007) and *The Architect's Dream of Winter* (2014).

Gerard Reidy lives in Westport, Co. Mayo where he works as an Engineer with Mayo County Council. His collections of poetry include *Drifting Under the Moon* (Dedalus Press, 2010) and *Before Rain* (Arlen House, 2015), shortlisted for the Pigott Poetry Prize.

Maurice Riordan was born in Lisgoold, Co. Cork, in 1953. He is a poet, translator and editor of a number of anthologies. His most recent collection of poems is *The Water Stealer* (Faber, 2013). He is the editor of *The Poetry Review*.

Mark Roper was born in Derbyshire in 1951. He studied in Reading and Oxford but moved to Ireland in 1980 to live in Tobernabrone, Co Kilkenny. *The Hen Ark* (Peterloo/Salmon)

1990 won the Alderburgh Prize for a first collection. *Catching the Light, The Home Fire* and *Whereabouts* are among his collections of poetry. *Even So: New and Selected Poems* was published by Dedalus Press in 2008. *A Gather of Shadow* was published in 2012.

Gabriel Rosenstock was born in 1949, in Kilfinane, Co. Limerick, "in postcolonial Ireland". He is a poet, playwright, haikuist, novelist, essayist and author/translator of over 180 books, mostly in Irish. He is a member of Aosdána and "Lineage Holder of Celtic Buddhism". His blog is at http://roghaghabriel.blogspot.ie/. A recent publication is *Antlered Stag of Dawn*, haiku in Irish, English, Scots and Japanese (The Onslaught Press, Oxford).

Colm Scully won the Cúirt New Writing Prize in 2014 and was selected for the Poetry Ireland Introductory Series. His first collection, *What News, Centurions?* is published by New Binary Press. A chemical engineer by profession, he makes poetry films which have been shortlisted in competitions in Ireland and the US, and shown at festivals in Kiev.

John W. Sexton was born in 1958. His poetry collections include *Vortex* (Doghouse, 2005), *Petit Mal* (Revival, 2009) and *The Offspring of the Moon* (Salmon Poetry, 2013). He was nominated for a Hennessy Literary Award. His poem *The Green Owl* won the Listowel Poetry Prize in 2007. He is a recipient of the Patrick and Katherine Kavanagh Fellowship in Poetry. *Futures Pass,* a new collection of poetry, is forthcoming from Salmon Poetry.

Eileen Sheehan was born in Scartaglin and lives in Killarney. She has published two collections of poems, *Song of the Midnight Fox* and *Down the Sunlit Hall*. Anthology publications include *The Poetry of Sex* (ed. Sophie Hannah), *The Watchful Heart* (ed. Joan McBreen) and *Text: A Transition Year English Reader* (ed. Niall MacMonagle). She is a former Poet-in-Residence with Limerick County Council; a new collection *The Narrow Place of Souls* is forthcoming.

Peter Sirr has published several collections with The Gallery Press, the most recent of which are *The Thing Is* (2009), winner of the Michael Hartnett Award, and *The Rooms* (2014). *Sway,* versions of poems from the troubadour tradition, was published in 2016. A novel for children, *Black Wreath,* was published by O'Brien Press in 2014. He is married to the poet Enda Wyley and is a member of Aosdána.

Gerard Smyth was born in Dublin in 1951. *The Fullness of Time: New and Selected Poems* (Dedalus Press, 2010) draws on four earlier books while his most recent volume is *A Song of Elsewhere* (Dedalus, 2015). With Pat Boran he co-edited the best-selling anthology, *If Ever You Go* (Dedalus Press, 2014), the 'One city, One book' choice for that year. A journalist by profession, he is poetry editor of *The Irish Times.*

Matthew Sweeney was born in Donegal in 1951. His most recent collection, *Inquisition Lane,* came out from Bloodaxe in 2015. A previous collection, *Horse Music* (Bloodaxe, 2013) won the inaugural Pigott Poetry Prize. In between were two pamphlets in 2014, *The Gomera Notebook* (Shoestring) and *Twentyone Men and a Ghost* (The Poetry Business). His *Writing Poetry* (Teach Yourself Series), edited with John Hartley Williams, is regarded as a classic of the genre. *Death Comes for the Poets* is his first novel. He teaches creative writing at University College Cork.

Richard Tillinghast was born in 1940 in Memphis, TN, but has lived in Ireland since 1990. His eight books of poetry include *The New Life* (Copper Beech Press) and *Selected Poems* (Dedalus Press, 2009). He has published three books of essays on Irish and American literature and a translation of the Turkish poet Edip Cansever. At present he divides his time between his native Tennessee and the Hawaii's Big Island.

Jessica Traynor was born in Dublin in 1984. Her debut collection, *Liffey Swim* (Dedalus Press, 2014), was shortlisted for the Strong/Shine Award. She is 2014 recipient of the Ireland Chair of Poetry Bursary and was nominated for a 2015 Pushcart Prize. She was named Hennessy New Irish Writer of the Year in 2013 and won the 2011 Listowel Poetry Prize. She was the 2010 recipient of a Dublin City Council Literature Bursary.

John Wakeman is a poet and founding editor of the literary journal *The SHOp*. His collection of poems *A Sea Family* was published by Bradshaw Books. He lives in Schull, West Cork.

Eamonn Wall was born in Enniscorthy and lives in St. Louis, Missouri where he is Smurfit-Stone Professor of Irish Studies and Professor of English at the University of Missouri-St. Louis. He has published six individual collections of poetry, as well as *Junction City: New and Selected Poems 1990–2015* (Salmon Poetry, 2015). He has written extensively on the subject of Irish Studies, his most recent volume being *Writing the Irish West: Ecologies and Traditions* (University of Notre Dame Press, 2011).

William Wall is a poet, essayist and novelist. *Ghost Estate,* a recent collection of poems, is published by Salmon Poetry. One of his novels was long listed for the Booker Prize, and he won the Patrick Kavanagh Award for his first poetry collection, *Mathematics and Other Poems.*

Grace Wells was born in London in 1968 and lives in Co. Tipperary. A former independent television producer, she has written prize-winning fiction for younger readers. Her debut collection of poems, *When God Has Been Called Away to Greater Things* (Dedalus Press, 2010), won the Rupert and Eithne Strong Best First Collection Award and was shortlisted for the London Fringe Festival New Poetry Award. Her second, *Fur,* was published by Dedalus in 2015.

Sandra Ann Winters is the winner of the 2011 Gregory O'Donoghue International Poetry Competition, and a Pushcart nominee, having won numerous poetry awards and commendations in her native US. She is the author of *The Place Where I Left You* (Salmon Poetry, 2014) and a chapbook, *Calving Under the Moon* (Finishing Line Press, 2013). She divides her time between Greensboro, NC and Millstreet, Co. Cork.

Joseph Woods was born in Drogheda in 1966. His first two collections *Sailing to Hokkaido* (2001) and *Bearings* (2005) were issued as a single volume, *Cargo* (2010) by Dedalus Press, who also published *Ocean Letters* in (2011). A former Director of Poetry Ireland he now lives and works in Zimbabwe.

Macdara Woods was born Dublin 1942 and has published more than a dozen volumes of poetry, among them *Collected Poems* (Dedalus Press, 2012) and *Music from the Big Tent* (Dedalus Press, 2016). He has been an editor of *Cyphers* magazine since 1975 and has also edited anthologies for Kilkenny and Mayo County Councils, among others. His work is widely published in translation and has been frequently set to music. He is a member of Aosdána.

Vincent Woods is a poet and playwright. *A Cry from Heaven* played at the Abbey in 2005, while *King Ubu,* his version of Alfred Jarry's *Ubu Roi,* was performed at the Galway Arts Festival in July 2006. *The Colour of Language,* a poetry collection, was published by Dedalus Press in 1994.

Enda Wyley is a poet and children's author. *Borrowed Space, New and Selected Poems,* was published by Dedalus Press in 2014. She has been awarded the inaugural Vincent Buckley Poetry Prize and a Katherine and Patrick Kavanagh Fellowship for her poetry, 2014. She is a member of Aosdána.

ACKNOWLEDGEMENTS

The poems in this anthology were first published or collected in the following books, and are reproduced here by permission of the publishers, authors or estates. All rights remain with the original copyright holders, to whom all requests for subsequent permissions should be addressed.

Graham Allen: from *The One That Got Away* (New Binary Press, 2014); Tara Bergin: from *This is Yarrow* (Carcanet Press, 2013); Eavan Boland: from *In a Time of Violence* (Carcanet Press, 1995); Dermot Bolger: from *The Venice Suite* (New Island, 2012); Pat Boran: from *New and Selected Poems* (Dedalus Press, 2007); Eva Bourke: from *piano* (Dedalus Press, 2011); Heather Brett: from *Witness* (Windows Publications, 2015); Paddy Bushe: from To *Ring in Silence: New and Selected Poems* (Dedalus Press, 2008); Rosemary Canavan: from *The Island* (Story Line Press, 1994), by permission of the author; Moya Cannon: from *Carrying the Songs* (Carcanet Press, 2007); Ciaran Carson: from *Belfast Confetti* (The Gallery Press, 1989); Paul Casey: from *home more or less* (Salmon Poetry, 2012); Philip Casey: from *Tried and Sentenced: Selected Poems* (eMaker Editions, 2014); Sarah Clancy: from *Thanks for Nothing, Hippies* (Salmon Poetry, 2012); Michael Coady: from *Oven Lane and other poems* (The Gallery Press, 2014); Enda Coyle-Greene: from *Map of the Last* (Dedalus Press, 2013); Tony Curtis: from *Folk* (Arc Publications, 2011); Pádraig J. Daly: from *The Last Dreamers; New and Selected Poems* (Dedalus Press, 2008); Kathy D'Arcy: from *The Wild Pupil* (Bradshaw Books, 2012); Michael Davitt: from *Seimeing Soir* (Coiscéim, 2004), *le caoinchead Joe Davitt* / courtesy of Joe Davitt; Gerald Dawe: from *Selected Poems* (The Gallery Press, 2012); John F. Deane: from *Snow Falling on Chestnut Hill* (Carcanet Press, 2012); Mary Dorcey: from *Moving into the Space Cleared by our Mothers* (Salmon Poetry, 1992); Theo Dorgan: from *Nine Bright Shiners* (Dedalus Press, 2014); Cal Doyle: by permission of the author; Martina Evans: from *The Windows of Graceland: New & Selected Poems* (Carcanet Press, 2016); John Fitzgerald: by permission of the author; Gabriel Fitzmaurice: from *A Middle-aged Orpheus Looks Back at his Life: New and Selected Sonnets* (Liberties Press, 2013), by permission of the author; Anne-Marie Fyfe: from *House of Small Absences* (Seren, 2015); Matthew Geden: from *Swimming to Albania* (Bradshaw Books, 2009); Rody Gorman: from *Sweeney: An Intertonguing*, an ongoing sequence (by permission of the author); Mark Granier: from *Haunt* (Salmon Poetry, 2015); Vona Groarke: from *Flight* (The Gallery Press, 2002); Kerry

Hardie: from *The Zebra Stood in the Night* (Bloodaxe Books, 2014); James Harpur: 'The White Silhouette' was commissioned by John F. Deane for *Poetry Ireland Review,* issue 112, reproduced by permission of the author; Michael Hartnett: from *Collected Poems* (The Gallery Press, 2001); Eleanor Hooker: from *The Shadow Owner's Companion* (Dedalus Press, 2012); Breda Joy: by permission of the author; Paddy Kehoe: by permission of the author; Brendan Kennelly: from *When Then Is Now* (Bloodaxe Books, 2006); Helen Kidd: from *Blue Weather* (Bradshaw Books, 2005); Noel King: from *Prophesying the Past* (Salmon Poetry, 2010); Thomas Kinsella: from *Marginal Economy:* Peppercanister 24, (Peppercanister Books, 2007); Jessie Lendennie: from Walking Here (Salmon Poetry, 2011); John Liddy: from *The Angling Cot* (Beaver Row Press, 1991), by permission of the author; Alice Lyons: from *speck: poems 2002–2006* (Lapwing, 2015); Aifric Mac Aodha: from *Gabháil Syrinx* (An Sagart, 2010); Jennifer Matthews: by permission of the author; John McAuliffe: from *A Better Life* (The Gallery Press, 2002); Joan McBreen: from *Heather Island* (Salmon Poetry, 2009); Thomas McCarthy: from Mr *Dineen's Careful Parade* (Anvil Press Poetry, 1999), by permission of Carcanet Press; Philip McDonagh: from *The Song the Oriole Sang* (Dedalus Press, 2010); Afric McGlinchey: from *The lucky star of hidden things* (Salmon Poetry, 2012); Iggy McGovern: from *The King of Suburbia* (Dedalus Press, 2005); Medbh McGuckian: from *The Flower Master and Other Poems* (The Gallery Press, 1993); John Mee: by permission of the author; Paula Meehan: from *Geomantic* (Dedalus Press, 2016); John Moriarty: by permission of the author; Aidan Murphy: from *The Restless Factor* (Raven Arts Press / Colin Smythe, 1985); Gerry Murphy: from *End of Part One: New & Selected Poems* (Dedalus Peress, 2006); Madelaine Nerson Mac Namara: from *The Riddle of Waterfalls* (Bradshaw Books, 2015), by permission of the author; Caitríona Ní Chléirchín: from *Crithloinnir* (Coiscéim, 2010), by permission of the author; Nuala Ní Chonchúir: from *Tattoo : Tatú* (Arlen House, 2007); Eiléan Ní Chuilleanáin: from *The Sun-fish* (The Gallery Press, 2012); Ailbhe Ní Ghearbhuigh: from *Tost agus Allagar* (Coiscéim, 2016), by permission of the author; Áine Ní Ghlinn: from *Deora Nár Caoineadh / Unshed Tears* (Coiscéim / Dedalus Press, 1996), by permission of the author; Doireann Ní Ghríofa: from *Clasp* (Dedalus Press, 2015); Mary Noonan: by permission of the author; Julie O'Callaghan: from *Tell Me This Is Normal: New & Selected Poems* (Bloodaxe Books, 2008); Eugene O'Connell: from Diviner (Three Spires Press, 2009); John O'Donnell: from *Some Other Country* (Bradshaw Books, 2002); Mary O'Donnell: from Those April Fevers (Arc Publications, 2015); Bernard

O'Donoghue: from *Gunpowder* (Chatto Poetry, 1995), by permission of the author; Liz O'Donoghue: from *Train to Gorey* (Arlen House, 2008); Mary O'Donoghue: from *Among These Winters* (Dedalus Press, 2007); Sheila O'Hagan: from *The Peacock's Eye* (Salmon Publising, 1992); Nessa O'Mahony: from *Bar Talk* (iTaLiCs Press, 1999); Mary O'Malley: from *Valparaiso* (Carcanet Press, 2012); Leanne O'Sullivan: from *The Mining Road* (Bloodaxe Books, 2013); Karl Parkinson: published in *The Level Crossing* (Dedalus Press, 2016), by permission of the author; Paul Perry: from *Gunpowder Valentine: New and Selected Poems* (Dedalus Press, 2014); Billy Ramsell: from *Complicated Pleasures* (Dedalus Press, 2007); Gerard Reidy: from *Pictures from a Reservation* (Dedalus Press, 1998); Maurice Riordan: from *Floods* (Faber and Faber, 1995); Mark Roper: from *Even So: New & Selected Poems* (Dedalus Press, 2007); Gabriel Rosenstock: first broadcast on *Sunday Miscellany* (RTÉ Radio 1), by permission of the author; Colm Scully: from *What News, Centurions?* (New Binary Press, 2014); John Sexton: from *Petit Mal* (Revival Press, 2009), by permission of the author; Eileen Sheehan: first published in The Irish Times, forthcoming in *The Narrow Way of Souls* (Salmon Poetry); Peter Sirr: from *Bring Everything* (The Gallery Press, 2000); Gerard Smyth: by permission of the author; Matthew Sweeney: from *Inquisition Lane* (Bloodaxe Books, 2015); Richard Tillinghast: by permission of the author; Jessica Traynor: from *Liffey Swim* (Dedalus Press, 2014); John Wakeman: from A Sea Family (Bradshaw Books, 2005); Eamonn Wall: from *Iron Mountain Road* (Salmon Publishing, 1997); William Wall: from *Farhenheit Says Nothing To Me* (Dedalus Press, 2004), is available for free download from the author's website at: *www.williamwall.net/ Freetext.html*; Grace Wells: *from When God Has Been Called Away To Greater Things* (Dedalus Press, 2010); Sandra Ann Winters: from *The Place Where I Left You* (Salmon Poetry, 2014); Joseph Woods: from *Cargo* (Dedalus Press, 2010); Macdara Woods: from *Collected Poems* (Dedalus Press, 2012); Vincent Woods: from *Poetry Ireland Review*, Issue 92, by permission of the author.

ABOUT THE EDITORS

PAT BORAN was born in Portlaoise in 1963 and has long since lived in Dublin. He has published a dozen volumes of poetry and prose, including *New and Selected Poems* (2005), introduced by the late Dennis O'Driscoll; the popular writer's handbook *The Portable Creative Writing Workshop* (various editions); the prose memoir *The Invisible Prison: Scenes from an Irish Childhood* (2009); and, most recently, *Waveforms: Bull Island Haiku* (2015). Editions of his work have appeared in several languages; awards include the Patrick Kavanagh Award and the Lawrence O'Shaughnessy Award for Poetry from the University of St. Thomas, MA. A former editor of *Poetry Ireland Review* and former presenter of *The Poetry Programme* on RTÉ Radio 1, he has edited numerous anthologies, including, with Gerard Smyth, the bestselling *If Ever You Go: A Map of Dublin in Poetry and Song*, the 2014 Dublin: One City, One Book choice. He is a member of Aosdána. See: *www.patboran.com*

EUGENE O'CONNELL was born near Kiskeam in north-west Cork in 1951. A primary school teacher by profession, he taught for all of his working life in St. Patrick's Boys School, Gardiner's Hill in Cork City where he now lives. He has published two books of poetry, *One Clear Call* (Bradshaw Books, 2003) and *Diviner* (Three Spires Press, 2009). His translations from the Latvian of Guntar Godins, entitled *Flying Blind*, and from the Hungarian of Lazlo Lator, *The Belling* (a collaboration with three other poets), were published by Southword Editions as part of the Cork European City of Culture Translation Series. He was invited to read with the Munster Literature Centre delegation to the World Expo in Shanghai in 2010 and by Culture Ireland to celebrate 'Imagine Ireland', a Year of Irish Arts and Culture, in the United States in 2011. A founding editor of the *Cork Literary Review*, he contributes reviews and articles to a number of publications. A *New and Selected* volume of his poems is forthcoming.

Dedalus Press

Established in 1985, and named for James Joyce's
literary alter ego, Dedalus Press is one of Ireland's
longest running and best-known literary imprints,
dedicated to contemporary Irish poetry and poetry
from around the world in English translation.

For more information, or to purchase copies of
this or other Dedalus Press titles,
visit us at **www.dedaluspress.com**.

*"One of the most outward-looking
poetry presses in Ireland and the UK"*
—UNESCO.org